Real Life Begins After High School

Facing the Future Without Freaking Out

Bruce & Stan

VINE
BOOKS

SERVANT PUBLICATIONS
ANN ARBOR, MICHIGAN

Vine Books is an imprint of Servant Publications especially designed to serve evangelical Christians.

Scripture quotations are taken from the *Holy Bible*, New Living Translation, © 1996. Used by permission of Tyndale House Publishers, Inc., Wheaton, Illinois 60189. All rights reserved.

Published by Servant Publications
P.O. Box 8617
Ann Arbor, Michigan 48107

Cover design: Left Coast Design, Inc., Portland, Oregon
Cover illustration: Krieg Barrie

00 01 02 03 10 9 8 7 6 5 4 3 2 1

Library of Congress Cataloging-in-Publication Data

Bickel, Bruce, 1952–
    Real life begins after high school : facing the future without freaking out / Bruce & Stan.
        p.   cm.
    Includes bibliographical references and index.
    ISBN 1-56955-155-3 (alk. paper)
        1. Young adults—Religious life. 2. High school graduates—Religious life. 3. Young adults—Conduct of life.   4. High school graduates—Conduct of life.   5. Christian life.   I. Jantz, Stan, 1952-   II. Title.
    BV4528.2.B535 2000
    248.8'3—dc21   99-086973

Printed in the United States of America
ISBN 1-56955-155-3

Contents

A Note From the Authors

This book is specifically and exclusively written to those students who have recently graduated from high school (or are about to). If that's not you, then put this book down. If it is you, then keep reading. You have your entire future ahead of you, but you've got to take it one step at a time. And those first few steps can be tricky.

Will you be stepping up the ladder of success or falling down the stairwell of failure? (OK, we pushed the analogy too far and got a bit dramatic, but you get our point.) Those first few years after high school can be sometimes terrific and sometimes terrifying. Actually, all other stages of life are terrific and terrifying too, but this book is about you and your future, so we'll stay focused on that age range of eighteen to twenty.

Let us say up front that we know what life after high school is like. Hey, we went through those years ourselves, and we have survived to tell about them. What's more, we each have two children, and all four of them have graduated from high school and are in college now. But don't think that the discussion in this book is restricted to our limited personal experience. Actually, most of what we talk about in this book is based on what we have learned by hanging out with people your age. In fact, that's how we met ... when we were both advisors to the college and career group at our church. But don't picture us as gray-bearded advisors; we prefer to be seen as hip, contemporary mentors. Also, we each have a pretty tight connection with a Christian college, so we are always around college-age men and women. We like it. It keeps us current with the kinds of issues you are dealing with in your life. Plus we get a better sense of style so we don't end up dressing like the stiffs who host CNN.

So, what you'll find in this book comes a little bit from us, Bruce and Stan, and a lot from the college-age guys and gals that we have known over the past few years. We even contacted many of them during the writing of this book and asked for some specific advice and "words of wisdom." You'll find their quotes sprinkled throughout the following pages.

A wise man (it was one of us, we just can't remember which) once said: "Learn from the mistakes of other people. You won't live long enough to make them all yourself." That's part of what this book is about: practical advice that you can use. Maybe what you'll read can save you a few dollars, a few hours, and a few embarrassing moments.

But there is more to this book than just practical advice and information. The most important part of our lives is our faith in God. That spiritual dimension brings balance, hope, and confidence to all other aspects and details of our lives. We can't honestly talk about your future without including God in the discussion. Actually, it is amazing to realize that God has a specific plan for you:

> "For I know the plans I have for you," says the Lord. "They are plans for good and not for disaster, to give you a future and a hope."
>
> JEREMIAH 29:11

If you are serious about making plans for the next few years, you ought to at least consider what God says about your future.

We are genuinely excited for you because we know that the next several years in your life are going to be a great adventure. You'll experience a combination of freedom, responsibility, learning, and recreation that won't be matched at any other stage in your life. With our help, maybe—just maybe—you can do it without ending up in debt, in the hospital, or in jail.

Bruce & Stan

Introduction

Because you are reading this book, you are probably a recent high-school graduate or at ieast counting the days that you have left. Since many of you are bigger than we are, we want to make sure you aren't insulted by the title: *Real Life Begins After High School*. We know that your life up to now hasn't been an imitation one. It has been real, very real. So where do we get off by saying that *real* life begins after high school?

For your first seventeen years or so, your parents and other adults dictate the circumstances of your life. In a big way, they decide where you will live, what you will do, and with whom you will do it. Oh, sure, you have your own personally selected group of friends, and you have freedom of choice to a limited degree. But let's be honest: it wasn't really your choice to spend the Fourth of July weekend at your Great Aunt Marion's house while she recovered from her bunionectomy.

By your eighteenth birthday and high school graduation, however, you enter an awkward transitional stage. We don't mean "awkward" in the sense of being uncoordinated and clumsy. (That happened in middle school. You have no doubt outgrown that stage and now move with grace and dignity— or at least without stumbling over the paint lines in the parking lot.) We mean "awkward" in a bizarre sense:

- The law says you are an adult, but your parents say you aren't.
- You are old enough to join the military and fire antiaircraft missiles, but your parents don't want you playing paintball because you might get hurt.
- The government will gladly take a chunk out of your paycheck, but the bureaucrats won't give you any respect because they think you're a "kid."
- You are in the target demographic group for new sports cars, but no

9

dealer will let you take a test drive without an "adult" to accompany you.
• Your parents tell you to assume more responsibility for yourself, but they feel compelled to remind you to carry tissues when you have a cold.

Exactly What You Didn't Know You Needed

What you could use at this awkward stage of your life is exactly what you don't think you need: advice. We're not talking about the advice your parents gave you during those lectures you didn't listen to anyway. We're assuming you already know:
• If everybody jumps off a cliff, you shouldn't do it.
• Don't drive without a seat belt; don't run with scissors; and don't step outside the house in just your underwear.
• Smoking cigarettes is a disgusting habit (even if it qualifies you to be a plaintiff in a multimillion-dollar lawsuit against the tobacco companies).

We're talking about advice on the part of life that you don't know yet:

You know a lot about what you know.
But you don't know much about what you don't know.

Let us show you what we mean. Take this little test to see if you are ready for "life on your own":

Question 1: Relationships.
   When is the best time to start a romantic relationship?
Question 2: Dorm Life.
   What aquatic devices are essential yet invariably omitted from every "what you need to bring" list?
Question 3: Finances.
   Where can you go for an all-you-can-eat lunch that is totally free?
Question 4: Health.
   What is the "Freshman Fifteen," and how do you avoid them?

Were you stumped by any of these? Don't feel bad. Your lack of knowledge doesn't mean you can't survive on your own; it just means you need to learn a little bit more about what you don't know. (OK, if you need to know the answers to these questions, turn the page.)

When your parents tell you these things: (a) you won't listen, or (b) they will be upset (or at least disappointed) if you don't follow their "suggestions." But not Bruce and Stan. We don't know you, and we haven't shelled out big bucks for eighteen years to keep you in high-fashion footwear and braces. So our feelings won't be hurt if you question our wisdom or scoff at our advice. But just in case you're worried that we might get a little parental on you, here's what we promise:

- *We'll be objective with you.* We've got no ulterior motives. Unlike some parents, we aren't looking to you to support us in our old age. So we don't have any particular career path already picked out for you. We don't care if your ideal job is to publish newspapers or just deliver them. We'll tell you the good and the bad and the pros and the cons without trying to influence you. We'll give you the facts as we see them, and then you can make up your own mind.
- *We won't lecture you.* There is no finger-wagging in this book. Our eyes won't bulge and our faces won't turn red as we tell you this stuff. We'll stay calm and serene. We have opinions, and we'll let you know them. But we know that *you* have opinions too. Unfortunately, we can't hear your opinions, but we respect them anyway. After all, we know it is *your* life we are talking about, and we'll assume that you aren't trying to mess it up on purpose. So we can't say that our opinions on everything are definitely right for you and that yours are wrong. Consider what we have to say as "friendly suggestions." That's how we intend it. You can take it or leave it.
- *We'll be user-friendly.* There is nothing worse than advice that is incomprehensible or inapplicable. So we'll keep it plain and practical. No theoretical philosophizing. We'll discuss the things that you'll encounter in everyday life.

Answers to the "Life on Your Own" Quiz

Here are the answers to the quiz from page 10.

Question 1.

Never start a romance shortly before a major romantic holiday. Otherwise, you'll have a terrible gift-buying decision. Think about it. If you start a dating relationship in mid-January, in a few weeks you'll be smack dab into Valentine's Day. If the gift is too elaborate, you might be viewed as moving too fast. If your gift is too platonic, you might be considered uninterested. Hey, you don't need this kind of pressure. Avoid all of this stress; don't start the dating relationship until February 15.

Question 2.

Water pistols are a must for every self-respecting dorm resident. And if you live on the second story or higher, then expand your arsenal to include water balloons. Don't think of these aquatic devices as a means of self-defense or as instruments of revenge. That would be juvenile. No, consider them a method of meeting other people.

Question 3.

Large grocery stores on Saturdays. You can graze for hours at the "free sample" food tables.

Question 4.

The Freshman Fifteen is a subcutaneous layer of poundage acquired during the first year at college and accumulated in the regions of the thighs, buttocks, and abdomen. In other words, it is fifteen pounds of lard. How to avoid it? Well, if you are eating at the college cafeteria, then resist the urge to put soft-serve ice cream on your oatmeal every morning. If you are in your own apartment, back off the macaroni and cheese.

What Kind of Book Is This, Anyway?

We hope that you find this book very helpful as you consider your future. We have designed it to be both practical and inspirational.

It's a Resource Book

We'll give you lots of helpful facts and statistics, Web sites, and information that you can use for college, living on your own, finding a job, and handling your money. But it's more. We don't just deliver sterile facts and information. We'll talk about things that are personal to you—the kind of person you are and the kind of person you want to become.

It's a Guidebook

You won't get all the answers for life in this book. (We don't even give you all of the questions.) But we'll try to get you prepared for life on your own by raising many of the issues you'll be facing. Like any good travel guidebook, we'll try to tell you ahead of time what you will encounter: points of interest, dangers, and customs.

It's a Devotional

From time to time, we'll direct your thoughts to spiritual matters. We'll ask questions such as: "Where does God fit into your plans?" We won't preach at you and we won't pass an offering plate when we're finished, but we hope that you find inspiration in this book to get even more serious about your relationship with God.

Most of All, It's Interactive

Well, this *book* isn't really interactive, but we are. We are anxious to hear your feedback. What did you find useful in the book? What could be tossed? Is there something with which you strongly agree or disagree in this book? Do you have insights and experiences of your own that other people could learn from? Well, let us know. We promise we'll personally respond to you. There are several ways you can contact us:

E-mail: guide@bruceandstan.com
Web site: www.bruceandstan.com
Snailmail: Bruce & Stan, P.O. Box 25565, Fresno, CA 93729-5565

Let us know how things are going for you at any point in the process.

Moving On

Well, you've been reading this introduction long enough. It's time to jump into the book and start thinking about your future. You can start right at Chapter One and go straight through, or you can skip around. It doesn't matter to us. You decide for yourself. You're getting ready for real life, so you better start making decisions on your own (although we'll admit that most decisions in your life will be much more difficult than deciding which chapter to read next).

Regardless of what some say, high school is not
the best time of your life. It only gets better.
And you should get better with it.

Lindsey B., age 21

CHAPTER 1

Custom Design Yourself—
Who Do You Want to Be?

Your graduation from high school has much more significance than the
decorative diploma that you'll receive (and that your mother will stick to
the refrigerator with a Hello Kitty magnet). That ceremony marks a new
beginning in your life. As you cross the stage after shaking hands with your
principal (and some anonymous school board member who mispronounced
your name), you'll walk through a hole in the space and time continuum, and
your life will never be the same. Soon you will:

- turn your tassel;
- attend more parties than you ever thought possible; and
- say "good-bye" and "let's get together this summer" to people you may
  not see again until the first reunion (if ever).

You'll find yourself reflecting on your past with mixed emotions. You'll feel both a sense of nostalgia and a little "good riddance."

Leaving Your Past Behind

Just when you've mastered the high-school thing, you are ripped out of the comfort zone of the old campus, the old teachers (and for some of them, we do mean *old*), and the friends you have had since kindergarten. You're suddenly thrown into the abyss of the unknown: Life *after* high school.

Before the panic sets in and you sign up for a second senior year, consider another perspective. Sure, it is scary, and we won't deny that initially your life will not be as certain as the "day-in and day-out" high-school routine, but think about the benefits of leaving all of that high-school baggage behind. After all, when you were going through it, you thought the routine was pretty boring.

Just think of the advantages of moving on with your life and leaving your past behind:

- *This is your chance to ditch the stereotypes you have carried around since middle school.* People won't care if you used to be considered a geek, a jock, or a deadhead. Their opinion will be based on your present performance and personality; their judgment of you will have nothing to do with the reputation you got in the seventh grade.
- *Your new friends will never suspect that you were once an ugly duckling.* They won't know that your appearance was technically augmented and visually enhanced by braces and "fat camp." (Just make sure you don't leave your high-school yearbooks lying around in plain view.)
- *That embarrassing nickname will be gone forever.* Nobody will be calling you "Little Patti Underpants" or "Tyler the Crier" based on some humiliating episode that you suffered in elementary school.
- *Best of all, you can create a whole new you.* The slate is clean. All previously established notions of who you are will suddenly vanish. Of course, maybe you won't really need an entire overhaul; perhaps just a little "fine tuning." But whether you want to scrap everything and start over or just make a few minor adjustments, now is your perfect opportunity to do it.

Two Questions for the Rest of Your Life

There are two questions that must be answered if you are going to take an active role in determining your future:

Who do you want to be?

What do you want to do?

We talk about the "who" question in Chapter Four and the "what" question in Chapter Ten.

Where Do You Want to Go?

When you were just a little tike, your mother probably laid out your clothes for you each morning. (In the last few years that hasn't been necessary because your clothes were probably already laid out ... all over the floor.)

The rest of your life was pretty much laid out for you, too. In high school, you had a few electives, but you had no choice about English, math, science, and gym. But now you are free from such rigid structure. Your future is not laid out for you. It is up to you to decide where you want to go.

Sans Plan

What if you decide to embark on your journey into the future without a plan? Well, we sure wouldn't recommend it, but it will take some pressure off you—for now. Planning is irrelevant if you have no destination in mind.

**If you don't care where you are going,
then it doesn't matter how you get there.**

In fact, you might be tempted to approach your future with a cavalier, care-free attitude. After all, your past few years have been pretty intense (with all the tensions associated with school, dating, working, parents, sports, and more).

Maybe you feel that you deserve a rest. Perhaps it seems both adventure-some and relaxing to think that you could just "wing it" into the future. But, believe it or not, failure to plan at this point in your life will probably make your life harder, not easier (as appealing as it may seem at this moment).

Now is the best time to gain the education and experience you'll need for certain jobs and careers. Think about it:

- *The older you are, the more complicated life will probably become.* It will be tough to go back to college when you are thirty-four years old, with a spouse and two toddlers. (It is no fun living in a college dorm if you have to miss the water-balloon fights because you are changing your kids' diapers.)
- *You won't always be able to live this cheaply.* You can probably survive quite nicely on a minimum-wage job right now, but that 1983 Ford Escort that you are driving has a limited life expectancy. Sooner or later you'll be wishing for a higher-paying job (or you'll have to be content with walking everywhere).
- *Some doors will close if you wait too long to walk through them.* It's too late to decide to be an astronaut, for example, if you are already collecting Social Security.
- *No time like the present to plan for your future.* Fifteen years from now, you don't want to be standing on the median at a busy intersection, asking for donations as the cars drive by, with a message scribbled on a piece of card-board that reads: "I didn't plan to fail; I just failed to plan."

Look Past Tomorrow

Your crystal ball is probably a little murky, but take a good look into your future. We don't mean the future of next week, or even next year. Look harder.

What do you see in your future five years from now? How about fifteen years from now? What do you see yourself doing? What kind of job do you have? Where are you living? What do you expect to be doing for fun with your friends? Are you involved with a church? Are you helping with any community charitable organizations? What is your family situation? How are you spending your money? We know these are tough questions to answer when the ink on your high-school diploma is still wet. But a little long-range life planning shouldn't seem too strange.

If you were planning to drive from San Francisco to Orlando, you would plan the route before you left. You wouldn't just hop in the car and drive east. Heading east without planning a specific route could land you in Boston (and you'd feel pretty foolish on the streets of Boston wearing those Florida resort clothes).

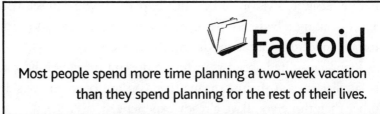

Factoid

Most people spend more time planning a two-week vacation than they spend planning for the rest of their lives.

A little long-range planning can keep you headed in the right direction. It helps you stay on course for the destination you want to reach. For example:

- *What do you need to study?* Don't declare a drama major in college if you want a career in biomedical technology. Plan to take those science, premed, and engineering courses.
- *What experience will you need?* A summer job as a beach lifeguard sounds great, but maybe you should plan to apply for a "gopher" job at an advertising agency if you are hoping for a career in marketing and public relations.
- *What relationships should you develop?* If one day you want to get married and have a close-knit family, then plan to get involved with groups where you will meet people with similar values. Think twice before you invest a lot of time with someone who has a tattoo that reads "Party Animal."

Are You Nearsighted or Farsighted?

Many people suffer from a vision problem that becomes a disabling handicap. We are not talking about eyesight difficulties. We are referring to a vision for your future.

Nearsighted. Guys and gals with a nearsighted vision of the future only see what is in the world immediately around them. The jobs they see in the future are the same jobs their parents have. Their view of the future is limited to the geographic region in which they have lived. Their future is restricted by what they can see in their present experience.

Farsighted. With a farsighted view of the future, you can see beyond your own experience. Maybe you have grown up in a large metropolitan center, but you can see the possibility of living in a small rural community. Maybe your grandfather was a physician, and your father was a physician. But if you have a farsighted vision of the future, perhaps you can see yourself owning and operating a bed-and-breakfast inn near Vail, Colorado (using the parlor for appendectomy surgeries during the off-season).

Being farsighted about your future doesn't mean you have to reject what is familiar to you. It just means that you are open to considering options other than those you have already experienced.

Made for the Job

Some people make the mistake of rejecting certain jobs and situations because they don't feel qualified or capable. They think that they wouldn't be as good as someone else who seems "made for the job."

The truth is, most people are not "made" for any job. (Notable exception: a gal six feet, five inches tall may be made for the WNBA.) Don't rule yourself out just because you think other people are better suited. You might be better than any person who is "made for the job" if you are more dedicated and work harder.

The best person for the job is the one who works hard enough to do the job best.

A Change in Priorities

Until now, your personal priorities didn't matter very much because you were living in a pattern that was determined for you by someone else. Lots of people were anxious to set the parameters of your life: your parents, your teachers and high-school administrators, your coaches or employers, even your friends. As you begin life on your own, however, you will find that you have the freedom to determine for yourself what is important to *you.*

So what *is* important to you? You need to decide this for yourself. Why is this important? We're glad you asked.

Lots of things and people are going to be competing for your time: new friends, your roommates, your college classes, your job. Other important parts of your life might get lost in the shuffle, such as your relationship with God, your parents, your siblings, other relatives, and your old friends. You need to determine *now* what is important to you, so you can make sure that important aspects of your life don't get overlooked.

Your Priorities According to Madison Avenue
Television advertising is geared to people in your age bracket. If you were to determine your priorities based on TV commercials, they would include:

Beer, always consumed around a bunch of jocks and swimsuit models, or by yourself in the serenity of the Rocky Mountains;

Cars, fast and flashy, or rough and rugged, with a low monthly payment you can't afford to miss;

Feminine hygiene products (too embarrassing to discuss); and

Casual clothing, to wear when you are swing-dancing with forty ethnically diverse fashion models in a windowless, all-white room or in a New York City alley.

Reality Check

Just for fun, take a moment to jot down six priorities of your life. This isn't like a pop quiz; it won't be graded. We just want you to try a little experiment. If you can, arrange them in the order of importance to you. To make it easier, we'll even give you a place to write them. Go ahead, we'll wait.

The priorities of my life include:

1. _____
2. _____
3. _____
4. _____
5. _____
6. _____

Now, check to see if those priorities are reflected in your life. Here's an easy way to verify whether you are living your life according to your priorities: Ask yourself these two questions:

- *How am I spending my time?* What you consider to be important to you probably isn't a priority unless you are spending time on it. If someone says you are her best friend, but she doesn't spend any time with you, you know that you aren't much of a priority in her life. Similarly, you might think that your relationship with God has a priority in your life, but that is doubtful if your only prayers are uttered during finals week. Where you spend your time is a good indicator of your priorities.
- *How am I spending my money?* You can learn a lot about yourself by looking at your checkbook ledger. Sure, most of the entries show money spent on yourself, and there is nothing wrong with that. Hey, you have to eat, and you can't walk around naked. But have you given any money to charity or ministries? Does your checkbook show that you are thinking of others or just yourself? You have a big inconsistency in your life if you say that education is a priority and your checkbook shows that you are spending mucho money at the video store three times a week.

The way that you spend your time, energy, money, and resources is the best way to discover your priorities. If you don't like what that tells you, then start doing the things that you believe should have more importance in your life. Once you have determined what is important, you can ignore the trivial things without feeling guilty.

- - - - - - - - - - - - - - -
**Things which matter most must never be
at the mercy of things which matter least.**
- - - - - - - - - - - - - - -

Goethe

Where Does It Go?

Here's a riddle for you:

> You have the same amount as everybody else,
> but you never have enough,
> and you always want more.
> What is it?

(Hint: Don't waste too much *time* pondering this question.)

As a high-school student, your daily schedule was regulated by a series of bells and buzzers. From the ringing of your alarm clock to the classroom bells at school, you moved through your day like Bobo the Monkey Boy, responding with the correct reflex action when you heard each noise.

Your life after high school will be a lot quieter. There aren't as many bells. That's the good news. The bad news is that it will be more difficult for you to stay on schedule. You won't have the regimen and routine of high school. You'll have much more freedom, and it will be your own responsibility to make sure everything gets handled on time.

If you are one of those who carry a personal digital calendar everywhere you go, then time management may not be a problem for you. But for most people, time management is one of the biggest challenges after high school. It is trickier than you think. There is so much that you will want to do. You have to learn how to distinguish the important things from the unimportant ones.

You cannot overestimate the unimportance of practically everything.

Once you have decided what is important and what is not, you need to schedule your day around the important things to make sure that they all get included. Once you have done that, then you can fill the gaps in your day with the unimportant things that you want to do.

A Time-Management Analogy

In the theater of your mind, imagine that you are in a science course at college. On the table is a pickle jar (not the normal size that is in the refrigerator but the kind at the wholesale club, about the size of your thigh). The science professor fills the jar to the top with stones (each about the size of a baseball) and asks the class if the jar is full. You reply, "Yes!" (Science has never been your strongest subject, but you are confident about this answer. You figure if you answer this question now, you can keep quiet for the rest of the semester.)

The professor gives you a look of disdain mixed with pity. He then pulls out a bucket of small pebbles from under the table. As he pours the pebbles, he shakes the jar so they fill in all the empty spaces between the stones. He asks you again if the jar is full. You were humiliated by your prior answer to his trick question, but you are staring at the jar that is jammed full of stones and pebbles, so you say, "Absolutely."

It is now obvious to everyone in the class that science is not your strongest subject. With a gleeful expression, like he just caught a rat in a trap, the professor brings out a bucket from under the table that is filled with sand. While muttering something about your insufficient cranial capacity, the professor begins pouring sand into the jar. It is amazing how much sand sifts between the stones and the pebbles. "Now," he says with an arrogant tone, "the jar is full."

There are two lessons to learn from this story. Lesson #1: If the jar was filled first with the sand, the stones and pebbles couldn't have been added later. Lesson #2: Don't answer a question in your science class unless you look under the table.

This story illustrates what you may need to learn about time management. The jar represents your life, then the stones are the important things that must be accomplished; the pebbles are significant, but not as crucial as the stones. The sand is just fun, "take it or leave it" stuff that has no real benefit. As you schedule your day, make sure the stones get in the jar first, and then the pebbles. Then the sand can fit in around everything else.

Time management can be a little tricky. Of course, it's easy when the decision is obvious:

- You skip the foosball tournament in the dorm because you have to attend your grandmother's funeral.
- Instead of sleeping in, you choose to attend your 8 A.M. World Civ class (most of the time).
- You ask your friends to postpone their trip to the beach for a few hours so you can work your full shift at the Fatburger drive-thru (because you don't want to jeopardize the chance to get your name on the "Employee of the Month" plaque).

But the correct decision is not always so obvious. Many of your scheduling conflicts will also require you to evaluate your priorities:

- You have to study for a test in your psychology course, and you have to write an essay for your literature class. You only have time to do one. Which do you choose? (Perhaps you should have skipped the Nintendo games yesterday. Too much sand in your jar.)
- You have been asked to be on a committee at your church to help the homeless, and you want to play intramural sports because it is the only physical exercise you get. With a part-time job and a seventeen-credit course load, something has got to go. What do you say "no" to?
- You are developing a romantic relationship that has serious long-term potential. The only quality time you can spend with your friend is on the weekend. You are offered a promotion at Fatburger that would require you to work long shifts on Saturdays and Sundays. Do you forsake love for a few extra bucks and all the fries you can eat?

The challenge in time management is not deciding between "the important" and "the trivial." It's in choosing between activities that are equally good or equally important. If you have a good grasp on your priorities, then you'll be better equipped to distinguish between what is good and what is best.

The enemy of the "best" is often the "good."

Just Say "No"

If you are a person who is usually over-committed, you have a time-management problem. It probably won't go away by itself. People will keep asking you to do things because: (1) you get things done, and (2) you always say "yes" when you are asked to do something.

Realize that the people who are asking you to do stuff can't see the "big picture" of your life. They may not be aware (unless you enlighten them) of your other commitments and therefore can't see that you are under so much stress that your hair is falling out and your gastric juices could burn through steel. For your own sanity, learn to say "no." You are too young to be bald and have an ulcer.

Bruce & Stan Help You to Say "No"

We know it is difficult to say "no" to people when they make requests of you. Hey, you want to be liked by everybody, so you don't want them ticked off that you turned them down. Usually you'll end up saying "yes" if you can't think of something else to say. So, if you get lip lock trying to say "no" when someone asks for time you can't spare, try these responses:

1. If I do that for you, I'll have to skip my meeting of Obsessive Compulsives Anonymous. And the doctor says if I miss a meeting, he'll have to increase my medication.

2. I'll be glad to help you out if you really need me. But I should be studying for my psych exam. If I get a poor grade and lose my scholarship, will you be willing to pay that part of my tuition?

3. Actually, I'm really stressed right now. I want to help you, but I'm on the verge of freaking out. FREAKING OUT! FREAKING OUT, I TELL YOU! (Then start banging your head on your shoulder, and walk away talking to yourself. Don't worry. Nobody will follow you.)

The Art of Goal Setting

Are you intimidated by the thought of assuming greater responsibility for your life? Does it seem overwhelming? Well, don't get discouraged. There are some definite steps you can take to get a handle on managing your life.

Step 1: Dissect Yourself

OK, put the scalpel away. This is about dividing your life into seven basic categories or dimensions:

- *Spiritual:* Your relationship with God.
- *Physical:* Your health and recreation.
- *Mental:* Your intellectual growth.
- *Financial:* How you spend and save your money.
- *Social:* Your relationships and activities with friends.
- *Occupational:* What you do to earn a living.
- *Familial:* (It sounds awkward, but it's a word.) Your relationships with your family members.

You are probably having mixed success in the different dimensions of your life. In some areas you may be doing fine; maybe others could use a little help.

Take God's Word for It

If you want to know what God has to say about the different dimensions of your life, check out these verses:

Spiritual: Jeremiah 17:5-8

Physical: Psalm 139:14

Mental: Proverbs 10:14

Financial: Proverbs 3:9

Social: Proverbs 13:20

Occupational: Proverbs 12:14

Familial: Ephesians 5:21–6:4

Step 2: Determine Your Objectives

In each of the seven dimensions, determine an objective for improvement. Even in the strong areas of your life, there is room for improvement. Since we don't know you personally (yet), we will make up four hypothetical objectives for you:

- *Spiritual:* Get to know God better.
- *Physical:* Fit into last year's swimsuit without little brother making whale noises.
- *Financial:* Save enough money for a car.
- *Familial:* Get along better with parents (so you aren't driving one another to thoughts of homicide).

Step 3: Set a Goal to Reach Each Objective

Once you have determined your noble objectives, you need to set a goal that directs your actions toward achieving those objectives. Objectives are usually general in nature, but goals are specific. Using the four objectives we picked for you, your goals might be:

- *Spiritual:* Read through the entire Bible, two chapters a day.
- *Physical:* Go jogging three times a week during the current semester to lose those "Freshman Fifteen."
- *Financial:* Save $3,000 over the next twelve months.
- *Familial:* Call your parents at least once a week. (This goal assumes you are living away at college. If you are living at home and you only talk to your parents once a week over the phone, forget goal setting and find a good family counselor.)

Look at what these goals have in common:

They are definite and specific. They say exactly what you expect to do, and the timetable for doing it.

They are measurable. You can keep track of how you are doing. Your $3,000 goal means that you will need to put $250 in a savings account each month. It is easy to check your progress.

They are challenging but not unrealistic. If a goal is unattainable, you'll give up before too long. That's why the goals aren't "two hours of Bible reading every day" or "jogging seven miles every day."

After you have set your goals, put them in writing and review them regularly. Don't forget to reward yourself when you reach your goal.

> ## Factoid
> Surveys show that only 10 percent of the population have goals, and only 3 percent have put their goals in writing.

You Are a Lifelong Project

You are an ever-changing, evolving creature. Now, we are *not* talking about Darwin's theory that a banana slug turns into a moose after a few generations. We're talking about the process by which you grow spiritually, emotionally, and intellectually as an adult.

Deciding who you are and the kind of person you want to become isn't a task confined to the age range of eighteen to twenty-one years. It is a lifelong process, but right after high school is a great time to get started.

Moving On

The first chapter in this book is devoted to discussing the kind of person you are and the kind of person you want to become. Before you go too far with your life after high school, you need to come to grips with your personal priorities and values. Whatever you believe, you will find people who will have contrary opinions and opposing views.

You will find the greatest conglomeration of philosophies and attitudes and beliefs on the college campus. Many people will be tolerant and accepting of who you are and what you believe. Others, however, will have nothing but hostility for viewpoints other than their own. Interaction with people who agree with you—and confrontation with those who don't—will be an important part of your life experience. Whether they happen in the dormitory, in the dining commons, on the quad, or in class, your discussions about the meaning of life will stimulate and challenge you.

Of course, there is a lot more to college than lofty philosophizing. In the next chapter we'll give you an overview of what you can expect.

> *Learn how to study.*
>
> John K., age 22

CHAPTER 2

College—Growing Smarter by Degrees

C ollege is an amazing thing. No other earthly institution you will encounter in your lifetime will have as much potential to impact, influence, mold, direct, discourage, energize, prepare, poop out, enlighten, frustrate, and change you—all in the space of a few years.

What Is College, Anyway?

In one sense, college is *tangible* because it is a place. When you tell people, "I attend Westmont College," or, "I'm going to Iowa State," they immediately think of a campus with buildings and trees and dormitories (even if they don't know where Westmont and Iowa actually are).

In another sense, college is *intangible* because in many ways it's a state of mind. When you tell people, "I'm a college student," they probably think of all the stuff you're learning. (They also wonder how much you're goofing off, but they won't mention this because they once went to college too.)

College is both a matter of
being in a state and also *a state of being.*

Right now college is something in your future, which is good, because you still have time to prepare (by reading this book, of course). Depending on how much of a planner you are, college could be a year or more away, or it may be right around the corner.

Maybe you're already in college. Someone gave you this book a few months ago (probably for graduation), but you haven't had time to read it until now, or you don't really have time now, but your brain is full of college stuff and you need a break. So you picked up this book, hoping for a little inspiration, or at least some reassurance that you did the right thing by going to college in the first place.

Either way we've got you covered! In this chapter, we'll help you prepare to go to college and we'll help you get through college once you're there.

Who Are We to Talk About College?
OK, you might be wondering what a couple of guys like us could possibly have to say about college that would be useful to you in the twenty-first century. After all, we went to college in the twentieth century (that seems so long ago). So even though we went to eleven years of college between us (Bruce raised the average because he went to law school), we aren't in college *now.*

However, we have something going for us that we think qualifies us to talk about college with you. We each have two kids (a son and a daughter each) in college *right now,* who were able to "coach" us on the intricacies of college life. Furthermore, we each serve on the board of trustees of the colleges our kids attend (and we don't even get a break on tuition), which means we have a unique perspective on what college is like and what you can expect.

A Brief History of College

The word *college* comes from the Latin word *collegium,* which means *college.* The word *university* comes from the Latin word *universitas,* which means *bigger than a college*. (We're only kidding, of course.) Actually, both colleges and universities are schools that continue your education beyond high school (prisons and reform schools do not qualify).

📁 Factoid

The oldest institution of higher learning in the United States is Harvard University, which was founded in 1636, only sixteen years after the Pilgrims landed on Plymouth Rock.

Generally, a college specializes in a particular field of study. The most common specialty for a college is liberal arts, which really isn't a specialty at all, but rather a systematic grouping of studies that includes natural sciences, social sciences, and humanities. Some colleges are known for excelling in one particular field, such as art, fashion, or architecture (sometimes these kinds of schools are called institutes).

A university includes several colleges or schools that deal with different fields of learning, such as law, medicine, business, psychology, and education. You can get a liberal arts degree at a university, but you also have the opportunity to do more specialized study in a field that interests you.

Colleges and universities have been around since the Middle Ages (when bloodletting was a popular major). The importance of higher education to societies and cultures around the world and through the ages cannot be overestimated. Literacy, scientific advancement, economic improvement, technological discoveries, Hacky Sack, and sports rivalries—all of these are made possible largely because of the influence of colleges and universities.

What If College Isn't for You?

"I've been working in my dad's construction company since I was old enough to tote a brick. It's what I want to do."

"I love working with cars. Someday I want to have my own shop."

"All I want to do is get married and raise a family. What do I need college for?"

When it comes to college, there are two basic viewpoints. The first is to view college as your ticket to a job, a career, and long-term financial benefits. Since you were a little kid, people (especially your parents) may have been telling you that if you want to succeed in life, you need to go to college. While we certainly don't want to disagree with your parents, we think there's more to college than preparing you to *do something*. The second basic viewpoint is this: college can also prepare you to *be someone*.

When you go to college, imagine yourself as a clean sheet of paper. The things you will learn, the friendships you will make, and the experiences you will have will all go onto the paper, so that when you emerge on the other side of your college years, your life will have more direction and purpose. Your goal should be to write a term paper with your life, and you should shoot for an A.

Of course, you may have some very good reasons for not continuing your education (or at least not going to college right away). Maybe you already know what you want to do and don't see that a four-year college degree would help you to meet your career objectives—especially in light of the debt you might incur in the process of getting that sheepskin.

Even so, don't discount the college experience too quickly. Even those who decide not to pursue a bachelor's degree may want to take a few courses or even earn an associate's degree to give them special skills for whatever they want to do, from running a business to becoming a nurse to running a home. (And don't forget that many young adults meet their future spouses in college.)

Above all, don't decide to skip college for the wrong reasons. "I don't like to study" isn't a good reason to avoid college. Neither is "I can't afford it." The truth is, you *can* afford college (see Chapter Seven). What you should be saying is, "Can I afford *not* to go to college?" (see Chapter Ten).

Where the Boys Aren't

Research conducted by *U.S. News & World Report* shows that women currently earn 57 percent of all bachelor's degrees. The U.S. Department of Education projects that by 2008 women will outnumber men in college by nearly three to two. While most high school girls have their sights set on college, an increasing number of boys are opting for jobs that pay well right out of high school, such as computer programming. However, the fact remains that male high school graduates earn an average of $23,000 less per year than men who go to college do.

"Not Now" Doesn't Mean "Never"

Maybe you just aren't in a position to be able to consider college right now. Maybe someone in your family has a serious health concern. Perhaps you plan to go in a year but want to spend a year serving God on a short-term missions trip. Or it could be that you started a high-tech company in your room while you were in high school, and you're about to be bought out by Microsoft (if so, keep reading).

Silicon Valley Likes College Graduates

With all the publicity about teenage technology millionaires, the truth is that the high-tech managers inCalifornia's famed Silicon Valley are big on college. The *Wall Street Journal* profiled an eighteen-year-old *wunderkind* who was making big bucks working for Internet companies while still in high school. Even though he could have increased his earnings as a full-time programmer, he followed the advice of his parents and bosses and opted for college. One manager said, "The college years add knowledge, maturity and polish. Besides, these kids will have opportunities for the rest of their lives."

There may be a legitimate reason you are choosing not to go to college right away. If that's the case, we'd like you to do two things:

1. Keep an open mind about the future, and trust God to show you if and when the time is right. (Our brilliant editor didn't finish her bachelor's degree until she was *twenty-seven.*)

2. Skip the rest of this chapter and go to Chapter Three. Even if you don't go to college right now, you still need to move on with your life.

If you're definitely going to college, or even if you're still undecided, read on. This is where it really gets good.

Bruce & Stan's Top Ten Reasons to Go to College

Your college years are unique. It's likely that you will never again have the opportunity to take three or four or more years out of your life for the sole purpose of pursuing your ambitions and dreams, not to mention eating junk food and staying up late. Never again will you be able to learn about life and how it works in quite the same way—stimulated and challenged by people who want to teach you, surrounded by others like you who are on the same path. And never again will you forge the kind of lifelong friendships you will develop while you're in college.

With these noble qualities in mind, here are our

Top Ten Reasons to Go to College

(some of these are more noble than others):

10. You can go for days without shaving and no one notices.

9. You can wear the same shirt for the entire semester and no one cares. (Provided you wash the shirt at least once a week.)

8. Better meatloaf than Mom's (don't tell Mom).

7. You can interact with people who can actually read and write (or at least send E-mail).

6. A college degree more than pays for itself because you'll get a better job (which you'll need to pay for those college loans).

5. If you aren't planning on getting a job, college still improves the quality

of your life. (Ever hear of an "MRS." degree?)

4. The contacts you make in college will affect you for the rest of your life. (Hint: Look out for those envelopes from the Alumni A$$ociation.)

3. College helps you to develop marketable skills (or at least better people skills).

2. College encourages you to reach for noble ambitions (like "do my own laundry and grocery shopping").

1. College football games are one of the few places where adults can spend their Saturdays screaming and sporting body paint in public. It's called "school pride."

What Are Your Options?

One of the big differences between your life up until now and your life from now on is *options*. For the last eighteen years or so, pretty much everything you've done has been planned for you ahead of time: the food you ate, the clothes you wore, where you went to church, where you went to school, what classes you took, and what you learned. About the biggest decision you've had to make in your life until now was whether or not you wanted fries with your Big Mac.

Well, that's about to change. You're an adult now (or you're almost there), and the world of options is about to open up to you in a big way, starting with college. The first option, of course, is where you're going to go to college. Let's look at the top options first.

Staying Home or Going Away

This is a major option requiring much thought, a thorough investigation, and many discussions with your family. Several factors affect the option of attending college in your hometown or going out of town, not the least of which is financial. In addition, you need to do an honest self-evaluation to determine if you are ready to leave home (of course, you aren't *really* leaving, not as long as you can bring dirty laundry home on weekends).

Many students prefer the option of attending a nearby junior or community college for the first couple of years and then transferring to a four-year college or university for the rest of their degree. This can be an efficient and cost-effective means of getting through college. Or you can go for a two-year associate's degree in any number of career fields.

It's important to get input from your parents (mainly because they may be financing a large part of your college education). Some parents find it hard to "let go," while others openly encourage their kids to leave home for college (don't take this the wrong way). We both believed that our kids would benefit from leaving home for college, and our experience has validated that belief. As much as we love having our kids around the house, we have enjoyed watching them grow and benefit from being "on their own."

Private or Public

Cost is probably the biggest factor in whether you attend a private college or the public variety. Every state has a college and university system that benefits resident students.

The cost of a private college education seems almost prohibitive to many families. On the other hand, many private schools will work very hard to help you find scholarships, grants, and loans. (More about college financing in Chapter Seven.)

Another factor you'll want to consider is that, in many public colleges and universities, it's very difficult to get the classes you need *when* you need them in order to graduate in four years. However, it's not uncommon for a student to earn a college degree at a private school in less than four years. Keep in mind that you can take summer school classes at your local public college, which can help you get some basic classes out of the way.

Finally, you'll want to factor in your own circumstances as you make your decision. It may be important to you to attend a particular school—either because of the program offered or because of its prestige. Maybe your parents graduated from an Ivy League school, and it's virtually expected that you will do the same. Tradition carries a lot of weight when it comes to choosing a college.

Big or Small

We talked to a high-school graduate who chose to attend a large university because of the athletics. It wasn't that she was going on an athletic scholarship. She just wanted to go to a school with nationally ranked athletic teams. That was important to her.

There are big differences between large and small colleges, and athletics is just one of them. You may think your high school was big with three thousand students. Well, that's considered *small* when it comes to colleges. *Big* is a university the size of a medium-sized town. The pace is faster, the crowds bigger, and the options greater. That may get your blood pumping, or it may scare you to death. You just have to investigate, which means talking to people who know the differences and personally visiting the campuses of your choice (see below).

Keep in mind that you will get more personal attention from your professors at a small school than at a large one. A fact of higher education is that the larger the school, the more common it is for teaching assistants and graduate students to teach undergraduate courses. In smaller colleges the professors generally teach the classes.

Christian or Secular

The fastest-growing category of higher education is the Christian college. More than a place to prepare for the ministry or to get training for missionary service, today's Christian colleges integrate the Christian worldview (you'll read more about that in Chapter Eleven) with a classic liberal arts education. There are even Christian universities that offer advanced degrees in business, nursing, computer science, psychology, and art.

Factoid

The enrollments of institutions that belong to the Council of Christian Colleges and Universities (www.cccu.org) account for about 1 percent of the total student body in higher education in North America.

There are ninety-three schools scattered throughout the country that belong to the Council of Christian Colleges and Universities. According to *U.S. News & World Report*, undergraduate enrollment at these schools increased by 24 percent from 1990 to 1996, compared with 5 percent at private colleges and 4 percent at public institutions.

Christian College Distinctives

Robert Kallgren and Bryan Beyer list the following characteristics of Christian colleges in *Today's Guide to Christian Colleges*:[1]

- Christian colleges provide a Christian atmosphere in which students can learn.

- They present a Bible and/or theological component in their curriculum.

- Christian colleges seek academic excellence.

A great Web site for gathering information on all ninety-three Christian colleges and universities in North America is www.ChristianCollegeSearch.com.

Should you consider a Christian college? We think you should (we admit to being biased, but in a good way). We're not saying that a Christian college is your only option, but it should definitely be an option, especially if you already have a Christian worldview. Today's Christian college doesn't shelter you from competing philosophies but rather shows you how secular ideologies compare to God-centered truth.

Still, more Christian students attend secular colleges and universities than Christian colleges. And that's not a bad thing. Our secular institutions need the influence and witness of Christian kids, and you may need the specialized training that a secular institution can provide. You just need to be ready, willing, and able to stand up to professors who will denounce your beliefs and students who will degrade your moral values (more about that later).

– – – – – – – – – – – – – – – – –

The American campus is very different from what it was 15 or 20 years ago—heavily politicized, doctrinaire, obsessed with race and gender, contemptuous of all things white and Western. Do the fresh-faced students and their parents have an inkling of what they are getting into?

– – – – – – – – – – – – – – – – –

Columnist John Leo on visiting five campuses with his daughter

Top Ten Ways the Bible Would Have Been Different If It Had Been Written by College Students

10. The Last Supper would have been eaten the next morning—cold.
9. The Ten Commandments are actually only five, double-spaced, and written in large font.
8. New edition every two years in order to limit reselling.
7. Forbidden fruit would have been eaten because it wasn't cafeteria food.
6. Paul's Letter to the Romans becomes Paul's e-mail to abuse@romans.gov.
5. Reason Cain killed Abel: they were roommates who disagreed over who would occupy the top bunk.
4. The place where the end of the world occurs: Finals, not Armageddon.
3. Out go the mules, in come the mountain bikes.
2. Reason why Moses and followers walked in the desert for forty years: they didn't want to ask directions and look like freshmen.
1. Instead of God creating the world in six days and resting on the seventh, he would have put it off until the night before it was due and then pulled an all-nighter.

Campus Visits

Visiting the top schools on your list, especially once you've applied to them, is essential. The college you eventually choose—even if it's local—is going to be your home for at least the next year and possibly the next four years.

Contact the colleges on your list and arrange for a visit. Colleges can't wait to show off their campuses and have you meet their students and faculty. You and your parents should prepare a list of what you want to see and questions you want to ask ahead of time.

It's essential that you take time to tour the local community as well. If you're going to live off campus, check out the cost and quality of housing. Safety is always a big concern for parents, both on and off campus, so ask about security issues.

When to Visit
Most colleges sponsor "Preview Weekends" for parents and students to come and look things over. These are great, but remember that if there's ever a time for a college to make everything look near perfect, this is it. Our suggestion is that you plan your own visit during the week (when classes are in session) and stay overnight, preferably in the dorm (this would be for you, not your parents). Talk to the students and ask direct questions. You'll get direct answers.

Making Your Final Choice

Ultimately you are the one who will have to decide where you're going to go to college. The best decision will come after you've done a lot of research, asked a lot of questions, and done a lot of praying!

Just in case you're still undecided, here are some wrong and some right reasons for choosing a college:

Bad Reasons to Choose a College
- Your admissions counselor was a "cool guy."
- The promotional literature and video were first-rate.
- A bunch of your friends are going there.
- The beach (or mountains or lake or Krispy Kreme Donut Shop) is less than thirty minutes away.
- This was the only school that accepted you (we're thinking of the famous line from Groucho Marx: "I'd never join a club that would have me as a member").

Good Reasons to Choose a College
- You discovered that the college has a strong program in your area of interest.

- You visited the campus, talked to some students and faculty, and even stayed in the dorm overnight.
- If you've chosen to attend a Christian college, you are confident that you will learn to integrate your worldview into your area of study.
- If you've chosen to attend a secular college, you are aware of at least one strong Christian ministry on campus and you've already found a Bible-teaching church.

Choosing a Major

Remember, you have lots of options available to you when you begin your college years. Don't worry about having a single focus when you start college. Use the first year or so to explore your interests. If you know what you want to do, that's terrific, but don't feel pressured to choose a major right away (being "undecided" isn't as bad as it sounds). If you happen to choose a major, only to change to something else, that's OK too. It's better to find out that you don't want to be an accountant *now* rather than after you've graduated and are working for a Big Eight firm.

If choosing a major is an area of great concern to you, go back and read Chapter One again, and then jump to Chapter Ten. It's more important for you to decide *who* you want to be—which is largely determined by your purpose in life—than to decide *what* you want to do. Besides, once you know who you are, figuring out what you want to do is a snap.

On Classes and Profs

The first couple weeks of college are going to be a major learning experience for you. You think you're going to arrive and be cool from the very start. You've got these mental images of yourself cruising onto campus with a certain attitude that says, "Look out, world, here I am." Well, get that image out of your mind and replace it with something that looks bewildered, befuddled, and completely out of sync. It's called a *freshman*.

A college freshman is one of the lowest forms of life, only slightly higher than pond slime. You're like a green recruit going into the Marines.

College administrators know this, of course, so they program your life for the first week or so.

You will stand in more lines and fill out more forms than you thought existed in the entire universe. You will go through registration, orientation, configuration, and probably deterioration. You'll move into your room and meet your roommate (more about rooms and roommates in Chapter Three), buy books, stock up on junk food, meet new people, and check out the neighborhood (scoping out the local Denny's for those future midnight runs).

You're going to feel like a complete dweeb, but that's OK. So will every other freshman. The good news is that you won't stand out because all freshmen are dweebs.

"Look, Toto, ... I Don't Think We're in High School Anymore"
Unlike high school, where Mom woke you up and made sure you got to school on time, no one's going to wake you and dress you and send you out the door with a lunch pail and a kiss on the cheek, not even your roommate (if this happens, get a new roommate). Unlike your parents, your college actually receives money on your behalf. In fact, the money is already in the bank, so they have nothing to lose if you don't show up for class.

You're on your own, kid. It's up to you to sink or swim.

The size of your school will determine the size of your classes, but even small colleges sometimes throw undergraduate students together by the hundreds in those so-called survey classes, such as "The History of the World 101," "Old Testament Survey," or "The History of Pots and Pans." It's up to you not only to show up for class on time but to develop good listening skills in these larger classes (staying awake is the first step to good listening).

Some students like to tape record class lectures while they doze off so they can listen later and take notes on what they missed. Bad idea. It's a far more effective use of your time (a precious commodity during your college career) to listen to the lecture the first time and take very good notes.

The Modern Professor

Unless you graduated from Sticks High School in rural Montana (if you'll pardon the redundancy), most of your nonsurvey classes will be smaller than your average high-school classes. This is so you can have close interaction with the new authority in your life, the college professor.

Without college professors, we wouldn't have college. You go to college to learn, and professors are the ones who teach (it's amazing how many brilliant insights we come up with). College professors are supposed to be experts in their fields of instruction, and for the most part that's true. In fact, you will find that most college professors are very dedicated to teaching you what they know so that you can graduate and be productive in your chosen field.

There are some professors, however, who could care less about teaching and really don't care about you. Somewhere along the way these people became cynical about life because they got mad at God or perhaps because they were dropped on their heads as infants. Their only joy comes from contradicting the truth and making your life miserable.

The Difference Between *Eccentric* and *Arrogant*

When it comes to your professors, learn to distinguish between *eccentric* and *arrogant*. An *eccentric* professor wears Birkenstocks, appears absent-minded, and mumbles to himself. But he still loves to teach. An *arrogant* professor doesn't care about your questions and ultimately doesn't care about the truth. Enjoy eccentric professors, but avoid arrogant professors like the plague.

Keep in mind that your college professors are the new authorities in your life. They know it and you should, too.

Don't Believe Everything You're Taught

A college professor worth his or her salt doesn't expect you to believe everything you're taught. Some professors love to make shocking statements just to stimulate your thinking. Try not to act shocked or offended, even if you're going nuts inside. *Think it through.* What is your professor really saying and why? Do your homework and ask questions. (Hint: Be inquisitive, but not annoying.)

If a professor says something that offends your beliefs, don't react emotionally and don't take it personally. *Think it through.* Respond clearly and in love, particularly if you are writing a paper.

Is It Possible for a Christian Student to Learn From a Non-Christian Professor?

Absolutely! In fact, you may learn *more* about your faith than you ever thought possible. Just remember that when it comes to papers and tests, it's possible that some professors will mark any answer even remotely connected to God as wrong. On the other hand, don't leave your brains in your room just because your professor is a Christian. God may be simple to accept, but he's a complex being with many mysteries. Avoid pat answers in any setting.

Study Habits

What can we say? We have four kids in college between us and, believe us, we want them to succeed at every level, especially in their courses. What that really means is that we don't want them to take any longer than necessary to get through college.

Ask anybody. The key to academic success in college, including graduating within the time you should, is studying. Even if you never studied in high school, there's no way you're going to get through college—at least not a college that gives a degree worth more than the paper it's printed on—without studying.

In college studying generally involves:

✓ Taking notes
✓ Reading
✓ Studying your notes
✓ Reading
✓ *Really* studying your notes
✓ Reading

Do you see a pattern here? College classes are mainly taking notes and reading. So learn to do both with speed and accuracy. Oh, and there's also a lot of memorizing involved, but good memorization is based on good note taking and reading.

Studying also involves actually going to class and staying awake. Woody Allen once said that 90 percent of success is just showing up. And when it comes to college, there's more truth to that than you know. Then, once you show up and take good notes, here's what you do with your assignments:

Do it now!

That's it. Very simple. Don't procrastinate. Cramming is okay, as long as you're reviewing. Cramming is not trying to do a semester's worth of reading the night before the test. That's stupidity.

Writing Papers

Papers are no big deal as long as you know how to write. If you somehow graduated from high school without knowing how to correctly write a paper, the best thing you can do is to take a writing class. We're serious!

Contrary to what you may believe, your computer can't write your papers for you. Face it. About the only thing your computer can contribute to your papers is a spellchecker, and even that is suspect. And if you're thinking of finding term papers on the Internet, forget it. Your professors are way ahead of you on that. Your stolen paper will stand out like a pimple on a supermodel.

In addition to a good grasp of basic grammar, writing good papers requires research. Get to know your library intimately. Learn how to find stuff and, whatever you do, don't plagiarize. Cite your references.

Taking Tests

Success in taking tests depends on good study habits. If your professor likes to give tests that require memorization, learn to memorize (we won't go into the techniques, but there are books and study aids that can help you).

Don't cram as a substitute for systematic study, and do your best to get enough sleep. Other test-taking techniques that may help include:

- Listening to Mozart right before you take your test
- Eating a candy bar
- Praying (but not as a substitute for studying)

You might even try talking to the professor about what to expect on the test (and we don't mean asking, "Is that going to be on the test?" after every other sentence in the lecture). Go up after class and ask your prof, or make an appointment. When your professor gives you some tips, write them down, nod knowingly, and look appreciative.

Taking Breaks

Later in the book we're going to talk about college and stress, because the two go together like cats and tuna fish. There may come a time in your college career when you need a break, like a semester or two. Just remember two things:

1. It's harder to start up again once you take a break, and
2. You can always take a lighter class load and stay actively enrolled rather than dropping out all together.

The experts say that the best time to take a break from college is not before you start college or while you're going to college, but after you *graduate* from college. Take a few months off so you can travel, think, evaluate, and plan for your future. Even if you have decided to go to graduate school, a break will recharge your batteries and keep you focused on your goals.

Moving On

In the next chapter we're going to tackle some of the issues involved in living on your own, whether you're in college or not. College can be a huge part of your life, but there's much more to these years than going to class and graduating. Remember that *real* success is more a matter of *who you are* than *what you do*.

I couldn't wait to leave home.
After I was gone for a while,
I couldn't wait to go back.

Abby T., age 21

CHAPTER 3

Forwarding Address—
Growing Up Usually Means Moving Out

If your home life is like that of most American households, there is a race going on in your family. The clock is ticking, and it is just a matter of time to see which happens first: Will you pack your bags and move out, or will your parents pack your bags and throw you out?

Your parents are getting on your nerves. Go on, admit it. That doesn't mean you're a bad seed, it just means that you're going through the natural growth process of becoming an adult and wanting more freedom. And since you're admitting things, why don't you admit that you are irritating your parents (as evidenced by those popped blood vessels in your father's eyeballs, and the fact that your mother is losing clumps of hair from her scalp). It's reciprocal. You're driving them crazy and vice versa. That is one reason most people think about moving out after high school.

You'll quickly discover, however, that living away from your family's home isn't as glamorous as it seems. Sure, you won't have someone imposing a curfew, or ordering lights out, or demanding that you turn down the volume on your stereo. You won't even have anyone telling you that pizza is not a breakfast food. But living on your own may also mean you are literally "on your own" for buying food, paying rent, cooking and washing, and a lot of other things that you never thought of before (because someone else was doing them for you).

Whether you are getting ready to move off to a dorm room at a university across the country, or you just want to move down the block to that basement apartment with a hot plate for a kitchen and a bucket for a bathtub, this chapter is for you. When you read what we have to tell you, you'll still want to leave home, but you'll have a better idea of where you want to go (and a greater appreciation of what you're leaving behind).

Life on Your Own

From the time you were a little kid, you have been saying, "When I grow up...." Well, that time has arrived. You *have* grown up. During the last four years of high school (more or less, depending upon your mental acuity or lack thereof), you gained a lot of experience with:

- *Human dynamics:* You've developed friendships and interpersonal relationships (of the social, romantic, and platonic types).
- *Finance:* You've made small amounts of money and spent slightly more than that.
- *Communicative skills:* You've created intricate excuses and presented persuasive rationalizations to your parents and teachers.
- *Cultural sensitivity and societal awareness:* You've watched a lot of television and movies.

With such worldly experience, it is no wonder that you are ready (even anxious) to leave the protective cover of your parents' roof and venture forth on your own.

Your efforts to move out may be met with one horrendous roadblock: Your Parents. You see, they have a totally different view of you. It all stems from the fact that they used to change your diapers. They still consider you to be something less than a real adult. All the experience that you gained during high school doesn't mean didley-squat to them. In fact, what you think qualifies you to be an adult is what they consider to be proof that you are still a juvenile:

- *Human dynamics:* They think you are hanging out with a bunch of morons.

- *Finance:* They say that you have been living off the allowance they have been paying you. (You are tempted to remind them that $5 per week won't even buy a meal at "Hot Dog on a Stick," but you actually need that financial subsidy so you can't afford to alienate them quite yet.)

- *Communicative skills:* They say your conversation with them is always limited to monosyllabic grunts (except when you fabricate elaborate and outrageous excuses when you are in trouble).

- *Cultural sensitivity and societal awareness:* They criticize you for watching a lot of television and movies (as if that is a bad thing).

But you do have something working in your favor: You are driving them crazy. They are tired of the refrigerator door being left open and the bathroom light being left on. They are losing patience with calls from your friends at 11:45 P.M. (That one is their own fault; they should have gotten you the private phone line you kept asking for.) They are totally frustrated with your habit of leaving clothes on your bedroom floor (which you think is efficient because time isn't wasted opening and closing the dresser drawers). These parental irritations work to your advantage. Even though your parents don't consider you to be an adult, by the time you're out of high school they are somewhat anxious to get you out of the house.

Give Your Parents a Reason to Let You Go

Are your parents reluctant to let you go? Tell them they aren't losing a child; they're gaining 120 square feet of bedroom space. Get them dreaming about what they can do with your room after you've left. Here are a few suggestions:

- *Indoor swimming pool.* All it takes is lining the floor and walls with heavy plastic sheeting and bringing a hose in through the window. Get them a few straws and tell them to blow bubbles if they want a Jacuzzi effect.

- *Billiard room.* Your dad always wanted one. Unfortunately, the measurements for a regulation billiard room are about twenty-eight feet by sixteen feet, so your bedroom is a little small. Tell them to use pencils (unsharpened) instead of cue sticks.

- *Isolation therapy room.* Paint the walls black and board up the window. Play soft music on the stereo (anything by John Tesh, it doesn't matter what; all his songs sound the same). Hang an "Herbal Breeze" car freshener in the closet. There you have it. It's a protected and soothing environment where your parents can go at the end of the day to release their stress and pressures. (You mom's hair will grow back, and your dad's bulging eyeball vessels will contract.) They'll love the tranquillity, and they'll soon be referring to it as "the womb room."

When to Go

When to make the break from your parents' home requires some strategic planning on your part. Like a great actor in a theatrical play, take your bow and make your exit at a time when the audience wants you to return for an encore. In other words, when you leave you want to make sure that your parents will let you come back. Let us put it this way: there is a right time and a wrong time to leave home.

It is the *wrong* time to leave when:

- You've just had a huge fight with your parents and Jerry Springer is calling to book you.

- You've just maxed out your parents' charge card and you need to vanish before the invoice arrives.

- You haven't had a meaningful conversation with your parents since the tragic news that Ginger was leaving the Spice Girls.
- You don't have anyplace to go.

It is the *right* time to leave when:
- You are in agreement with your parents that it is the right thing to do.
- There are no hard feelings between you and your parents.
- You are just beginning to consider their antiquated opinions to be "quaint," and they are just beginning to consider your irritating habits to be "endearing."
- You've got a great place to go.

The departure usually happens when you start college as a first-year student, but the specific timing will be determined by a lot of factors.

But I Don't Want to Go!
What if you don't want to leave home? Well, you probably don't have to, at least not yet. But part of your growth process means stepping out in the world. That usually means living farther away from your parents than the bedroom across the hall.

What to Take With You

For the past eighteen years, all your worldly possessions have been stockpiled in your room. This arrangement was due to necessity (your parents didn't want your junk in the living room) and perhaps to protection (you didn't want your younger siblings getting their grubby little hands on your stuff). When you leave home, you will be tempted to take all of your stuff with you. Don't. You won't need it all, and you won't have room for it anyway.

This section is pretty simple. We just want to give you a few pointers to get you started sorting and packing. If you need a more detailed plan for the actual event of moving out, talk to your mother. Or buy a book like Peterson's *Ultimate College Survival Guide*.

What to Leave Behind
We know that you are fond of that soccer trophy you won in the fifth grade, but that is a remembrance of the past that can stay behind. And if you are honest with yourself, you aren't all that sentimental about it (since for the last year you had a Jack-in-the-Box antenna ball stuck on the soccer player's head). Your dorm room or apartment won't be much bigger than those photo booths at the mall where you can get four shots for a buck. With that in mind, plan to leave at home things such as:
• your high-school yearbooks;
• your collections from childhood (such as comic books and troll dolls);
• your favorite clothes from tenth grade that you haven't worn since; and
• your pets (goldfish might be the only exception, but not in that thirty-gallon aquarium).

In a word, pack light (OK, that's two words). If you are just moving a short drive away to college, you can always go back to get what you need. (And if you are going so far away that you won't return home until summer break, then you *really* need to minimize nonessentials.)

Rule of Thumb #1
If you haven't actually used it in the last three months, you don't need to take it with you.

Rule of Thumb #2
Don't take more than you can pack in one vehicle; your dorm room or apartment isn't going to be much bigger than the inside of a Yugo.

What to Take

If you are going away to college, you will probably receive information from your college or university about what you should bring. The obvious things will be on the list: a desk lamp for reading, computer, surge protector, your own towels and bed sheets (hey, you aren't staying at the Marriott Courtyard), and headphones for your stereo so you won't disturb your roommate.

There are going to be a lot of things you haven't needed at home that you will need at college:

- *A laundry basket.* The washers and dryers aren't going to be forty feet away like at home; you might have to walk down a few hallways and several flights of stairs. You don't want to be dropping any of your "delicates" along the way.

- *A small refrigerator.* Midnight snacks are easy at home when your room is only twelve giant steps away from the kitchen. But if the dining commons at college is across campus and closes at 8 P.M., the growling of your stomach may keep you awake at night unless you find some way to feed the beast within you.

- *An electric fan.* Many older college dorms are not equipped with air conditioning. A fan will keep your room cooler—and help dissipate the odor of the pile of dirty laundry in your closet.

- *A small tool set.* We don't mean a set of tiny tools; we mean just a few basic tools: a hammer, screwdrivers (flathead and Phillips), and pliers should be enough to get you started.

Coordinate this equipment list with your roommate. There is no sense duplicating items.

Scavenger Hunt (the Play-at-Home Version)

Consider the "little" things you will need when you move off to college or to your first apartment. For example:

- *school supplies:* paper, pens, printer cartridges;

- *kitchen stuff:* dishwashing basin and dish soap (good for washing delicates, too), knives, spoons, forks, coffee maker, coffee mugs, large popcorn bowl, and a few smaller bowls and plates;
- *laundry supplies:* detergent, fabric softener, stain remover, iron;
- *bathroom supplies:* vitamins, soap, shampoo, other hair stuff, toothbrush, and toothpaste; and
- *snack foods:* chips, cereal, granola bars, dried fruit, popcorn, cookies.

These things can be expensive if you have to purchase them all at once. A cost-free alternative would be a "scavenger hunt" through your parents' pantry, laundry cabinets, and desk before you leave.

Dorm Life

College is going to be filled with a lot of adjustments for you. As we mentioned earlier, you are going to be reading more and studying harder than you did in high school. But the academic transition is going to be easy compared to the tremendous adjustment to living in a dorm.

Think about it for a moment. Nothing in your lifetime of experience has equipped you for living in a dorm (unless you have 179 brothers and sisters).

A New Type of Home Life
You'll have to make a number of adjustments ... and quickly:

- *Instead of an older brother or sister, you'll have an RA (resident assistant).* The RA will probably be a junior or senior. This person is paid to be your supervisor, mentor, counselor, and warden. But don't think RAs are doing it only for the money. They usually get free room and board instead of cash. If you work that out on an hourly basis, their pay is about twenty-seven cents per hour. So they're probably doing this job because they want to be helpful.

  Take advantage of your RA's knowledge and experience. They know the really important stuff about college that you won't find written in the catalog (like which professors to avoid and what pranks you can play without getting into too much trouble).

- *Instead of parents, you will have an RD (resident director).* This could be a little old lady or a graduate student. The RD is your best resource for heavier personal problems. (Your RA is OK, but not much older than you, so you might want to opt for a little more wisdom.)
- *Minimal privacy.* Instead of sharing the bathroom with one or two siblings, you'll be looking at an average of about sixteen persons per toilet. You do the math.
- *Minimal quiet time.* We're not talking about your morning devotions here. Instead of a "lights out" rule imposed by your parents, there will likely be activity throughout the night. At first you'll probably join in on the fun, but after four months of sleeping only three hours per night, your brain won't function and you will be constantly sick. (But don't worry about that runny nose; the bags under your eyes will be so droopy that you can wipe your nose with them.)

Roommate Roulette

Dorm life is a lot like summer camp, only with homework. It's a great experience (for a few years at least), but there are a few practical pointers to consider when it comes to the person who will share your living space—your roommate.

It is possible that you will go off to college with a friend you want to room with. That is the exception. For most first-year students, your roommate is somebody that you don't know until you move in on that first day. The Housing Office at the college will make the roommate assignments. This is not a totally random process. It works a bit like a computerized dating service (without the romance element).

Sometime during the spring or summer preceding your first year, the college will send you a questionnaire about your living habits. The questions will be something like this:

Which word best describes your bedroom at home:
(a) clean, (b) cluttered, or (c) toxic waste.

What kind of music do you listen to:
(a) rock, (b) alternative, (c) contemporary Christian, or (d) classical.
(If you listen to Broadway musicals, you have to live by yourself off-campus.)

Would you describe yourself as a:
(a) loner, (b) social butterfly, or (c) party animal.

Describe your sleeping habits:
(a) early bird, (b) night owl, or (c) hibernating bear.

This may be the only college test that you can answer perfectly. But don't think that it is easy. You will be tempted to change your answers based on the kind of person you hope to become ("I never did any homework in high school, but I'm sure I'll be studying thirteen hours every day at college") or based on the kind of person you want for a roommate ("Well, I'm a slob, but I sure don't want a roommate who is one, so I'll tell the college that I am a neat freak").

Survival Tips

A few weeks before the beginning of your first semester, you will be notified of the name, address, and phone number of your roommate. Spend some time on the phone getting to know each other. Don't worry if you think you got stuck with a dud (your new roommate probably has a similar feeling). Don't even think about asking for a change in roommate assignments until you have both moved in and gotten to know each other.

There is one exception to this general rule: if your future roommate asks, "Do you want to bring your drum set, or should I bring mine?"

You may be apprehensive about living with a complete stranger, but your roommate won't stay a stranger for long. Sure, you won't be totally compatible, but you lived at home and weren't totally compatible with your family members, either.

Even if you shared a room with a sibling, the experience won't completely prepare you for living with a roommate. The rules for living with a roommate are slightly different. At home, your parents can arbitrate the disputes with your siblings; at college, you'll have to work things out on your own with your roommate. The following perspectives may help:

- *Don't think that your roommate has to be your best friend.* That will be nice if it happens, but it probably won't. You are likely to find your best friends in classes or activities on campus. Just because you share the same alarm clock and bulletin board doesn't mean that you have to be inseparable.
- *Learn to appreciate your roommate's differences.* At home, you're living with people who do things the same way and have similar habits and customs. But your roommate may come from a different part of the country or from a different background. You may be hearing different expressions (what is a "soda" in the Northeast is "pop" in the Midwest), or an accent, or eating habits (one of you may never have eaten grits, and the other may not know the difference between an artichoke and an avocado).
- *Don't be too quick to borrow your roommate's stuff.* Sure, when you are living at home, anything in anyone's closet is communal property. You can borrow your brother's sweatshirt, and he'll use your ski gloves. And your dad's closet is good for ... well, there's not much in there that is in style, but the ties are good if you are going to a seventies party. Your roommate may be a little more protective. Don't just assume that you can wear and use the stuff that isn't yours.
- *When your roommate is starting to irritate you, remember that you may be doing things that irritate your roommate.* Yes, we know that seems inconceivable, but it is true. Your parents have to think that your little quirky habits are "cute" because you are their offspring. Everyone else might find your habits to be annoying. You could be bothering your roommate, and you might not even know it. Maybe it is the way you stack the cotton swabs in the shape of a log cabin after you have used them in your ears. You might think this reveals your aptitude for engineering, but your room-

mate probably finds it disgusting (and, quite frankly, so do we). Learn how to tactfully discuss these things with each other.

- *Don't let the irritations build up to a point where you explode over something ridiculous* (such as "I hate you, I hate you ... You always hum when you comb your hair!").

Sharing a room with someone requires both courtesy and compromise. These are essential qualities that you will need later in life (particularly if you are going to be married).

Dining Commons

When you are at college, you'll probably eat most of your meals in a dining commons along with hundreds of people just like you. In Chapter Eight we'll discuss some guidelines for *what* to eat (so you don't swell like an overinflated whoopee cushion after the first semester). For now, we just want to remind you that table manners seem to be forgotten when people eat in scavenging hordes.

We are not being critical, just observant. We know that you'll be foraging for food in a cafeteria line and eating off a tray. This is not a time to be lifting your pinkie as you sip your soup. But when you go home, or get invited to the university president's house for dinner, don't toss the peas into the air and catch them in your mouth.

Lavatory Lunacy

There will be enough toilets, sinks, and showers in your dorm to accommodate all of the residents—enough, that is, if everyone goes to the bathroom at a different time throughout the day. But that is not real life. Like the rush-hour traffic commute, there is going to be a logjam at the porcelain turnoff every morning and every night. You might have to arise a little earlier, or go to bed a little later, if you want the luxury of an extended shower (or at least hot water).

Scheduling Problems

We don't know when you'll want to study. Maybe you'll want to do it in the afternoon; maybe you'll want to do it in the evening. But know that whatever time you choose, there will be a conflict with someone in the dorm who owns the largest set of stereo speakers. And when you want to get a little crazy, you can bet that your roommate will be sick, or asleep, or studying (actually, sometimes the sleep and studying modes tend to overlap).

A Little Privacy, Please ...

In order to maintain your sanity, you are going to have to find your own little, private "quiet place." This will be a place where you dodge all of the interruptions. It will be your place where you can talk with God and read your Bible; it will be a place where you can organize your thoughts; it will be a place where you enjoy the quietness of silence. (And maybe you do a little homework here too.)

It may take you a while to find this special place. Look for an isolated, over-stuffed chair in the library. Try to find a bench under a shade tree (preferably far away from the soccer practice field). If all else fails, try the backseat of your RA's car. Wherever it is, find this place and don't tell anyone about it until after you graduate.

Apartment Life

Life in an apartment has some similarities to living in a dorm, but there are some significant differences:

Furniture
Dorm rooms come furnished with beds and dressers and desks. Unless you rent a place that is furnished, the only features of your apartment will be wall-to-wall floors and see-through windows. You will be on your own for the furniture.

Your vivid imagination and your empty wallet will guide your decorating tastes. Who needs a bed frame when a mattress lies perfectly flat on the floor? The box that your seventeen-inch computer monitor came in will make an excellent dining table. If you get really desperate for furniture, invite your parents over for dinner at your apartment. When they have to sit on a six-pack of Diet Coke instead of a chair, they may take pity on you.

You'll be amazed at what you can build out of "sticks and stones." A few pine boards (about twelve inches wide and six feet long) stacked between concrete bricks make an excellent bookcase. Or, if you want to go for the beachcomber motif, build two towers of bricks and lay a surfboard across the top. Presto! You've got an abstract breakfast counter.

Neighbors

Dorms are going to be populated exclusively with college students. That may not be the case with an apartment. Check out the neighbors when you are apartment hunting. If you plan to listen to your stereo and have friends over after 8:00 P.M., don't get an apartment in the seniors' village. Conversely, if you hope to study in your apartment, then don't rent the one located above the "All-Nite Tattoo Parlor."

Location, Location, Location

You might find a great apartment for a great price, but you'll have a problem if it is seven miles from campus and your only means of transportation is a pair of Nikes. Dorms are always conveniently located, but that may not be the case with an apartment.

Remember that your college classes are not scheduled in a row like in high school. You might have only two classes on Monday, Wednesday, and Friday, but one is at 9:30–10:20, and the other is 1:15–2:05. Where are you going to go in the meantime? If your apartment is too far away, you might have a lot of wasted time between classes when you can't conveniently eat, sleep, shower, or study. And if you have a car, then you have to worry about parking (both at the apartment and on campus).

For your first year at college, living closer to campus is probably better than being farther away. Not only is it more convenient, but you'll also be able to participate in more of the social activities.

The Wonderful World of Laundry

Maybe Mom spoiled you and did all your laundry. Maybe you walked through the laundry room only to get to the garage. Well, all of that is going to change when you go away to college. Once you are on your own, you have only three options:

- *Option 1:* Go home often (and if you greet your mom with a big kiss, maybe she'll wash all of those clothes you've crammed into your duffel bag).
- *Option 2:* Do the wash yourself in the dorm or at the laundromat.
- *Option 3:* Wear stinky clothes.

If you think Option 2 might cramp your social life too much, remember that you won't have any social life if you are always going home or if your clothes dispense a scent that makes people's eyes water.

Do You Have What It Takes?
If your mom wanted to prepare you for the "real world," you have been doing your own laundry at home for quite a while. But don't think for a moment that doing laundry at college will be the same as folding and fluffing at home. That is like comparing Marine boot camp to summer church camp.

In the laundry room at home, all the detergent, softener, and cling-free static sheets are in the cupboard. There won't be any of those products in the dorm laundry room or at the laundromat. You'll have to bring your own. Most important of all, you'll need plenty of quarters (and not for the candy-vending machines); you'll be feeding quarters into washers and dryers faster than a little old lady at a casino slot machine.

Laundry Room Larceny
Speaking of Marine Corps boot camp, you'll need to acquire some commando skills if you want to protect your clothes from theft or sabotage. You'll have to be on constant sentry duty. If you leave your clothes unguarded, laundry terrorists will toss your clothes out of the washer and put their

clothes in faster than you can say "spin cycle." If you return just a few minutes late, the culprit will have vanished, and you'll be staring at your pile of sopping wet undies on the concrete floor.

Even if you are successful in making it through the wash cycle, you still have to stay on guard during the drying process. If you don't pick up your clothes as soon as the dryer cycle is finished, someone who needs the dryer will take them out for you. Your freshly cleaned and dried clothes will be dumped on the floor. Your nice things will then be stolen, and the rest of your clothes will absorb some unknown fungus for which there is no cure.

Pumping Iron

If you're lucky, the dorm laundry room will have one or two irons and ironing boards. You might think that this is a disproportionately small supply for the hundreds of people living in the dorm. Not so, because most college students don't iron their clothes. That's why the "casual look" is so popular on college campuses—not because it's stylish, but just because no one wants to go through the hassle of ironing. College students have too many other commitments that are, shall we say, pressing.

So when you are shopping for clothes at the mall before you go away to college, roll all of the clothes in a ball and wrinkle them before you try them on. You've got to see how the clothes look when they are crumpled if you want to know what you'll look like when you wear them on campus.

A Final Word of Caution for When You Leave Home

Before you make the official and final departure from your parents' house, take a good look around. For the first time you may notice the nice furniture, the clean surroundings, and the well-stocked refrigerator. Don't make the mistake of asking your parents: "Why should I leave all of this?" One of them will quickly answer: "Because it is not yours!"

Moving On

When you are living in your parents' home, you play by their rules. Sometimes it is difficult to know "who you really are" when you're in that situation. What you think, do, and say is strongly influenced by your parents' expectations.

All of that changes when you move away from home. Suddenly what you think, do, and say is totally up to you. Your parents no longer dictate these things; your character determines them. That important subject, your character, is the focus of the next chapter.

After high school, you'll find out what you *really* believe because then it is all up to you.

Carolyn C., age 20

CHAPTER 4

Your Character—
It's Who You Really Are

After high school, it may feel as though you don't know who you are any-more.

Don't freak out. It isn't all bad, just part of the process. For eighteen years you have been defined mostly by what your family does and says and believes. You have also been partly defined by the friends you hang around with. After high school, and particularly if you go away to college, you won't have your family and old friends around to define you. Your external environment may be different.

But you are still the same person inside.

That can be hard to remember when everything starts changing so sud-denly and drastically. The activities in your life will increase exponentially after high school. Unless you are careful, the "inner you" may get lost, or at least overlooked. If you're going to college, then the academic load will almost bury you; if you're working a job, you'll be physically and emotionally drained at the end of the day. If any time is left between your classes and your job, you'll be doing things and going places with your friends. In the midst of the flurry of activity, don't ignore the importance of developing your character.

The tough decisions in your life are not going to be decided by your looks, or your personality, or your intellect. The most difficult issues you'll face in life are going to be decided by your character.

What Is Character?

Character is the inward conviction of your beliefs that affects your outward behavior. Your character is the "real you." It is what you stand for—what you believe in. Your character is what may keep you from doing things you shouldn't, and it makes you do the right thing even when it is difficult.

What Does Character Look Like?

Unfortunately, you can't see character. You can't take a written test to quantify it. You will only know what your own character is like by examining your conduct in various circumstances. Your character is revealed by:

- how you treat people who can do nothing for you
- your ability to accept personal criticism without feeling malice toward the person who gives it
- your response when you suddenly lose a lot of money—and when you suddenly acquire a lot of money
- the kinds of things that make you angry
- the kinds of things that make you laugh
- how you respond to temptation
- what you stand for and what you won't stand for

- what you fall for and what you lie for
- what you do with what you have
- wnat you do when you have nothing to do
- what you do when you know nobody will ever find out

- - - - - - - - - - - - - - - - -
Reputation is what you need to get a job.
Character is what you need to keep it.
- - - - - - - - - - - - - - - -

Essential Ingredients

During high school, there were probably times when your character was tested. As difficult as those circumstances might have been, the temptations and pressure to compromise your character will increase dramatically after high school. You need to be serious about developing and strengthening your character so that you will be able to stand firm in the confidence of what you believe.

Some men and women are universally recognized for their character (such as Billy Graham and Mother Teresa). These people are known for consistently exemplifying sound moral character. If you find it hard to imagine living up to such lofty standards, take heart. Character is not something acquired genetically; nor is there a "one-size-fits-all" formula for character development. It takes time ... and a fair amount of effort.

Where to begin? Well, this list of desirable character traits is not intended to be exhaustive, but if you are working on your own character, these are good traits to start with:

- *Integrity:* Doing what is right.
- *Honesty:* Being truthful.
- *Responsibility:* Being trustworthy.
- *Morality:* Being pure in thought and deed.

There Is More to the Definition

Look at the brief definitions that we have given to the character traits of integrity, honesty, responsibility, and morality. Now, for each one of them, add the following phrase: "all of the time, in every situation, regardless of the consequences." This is what *character* is all about.

Character is always lost when a high ideal is sacrificed on the altar of conformity and self-interest.

Sometimes it is easier to exhibit character when faced with big temptations than it is when faced with seemingly insignificant ones. If a bank teller left a stack of twenty-dollar bills on the counter, we could resist the momentary temptation to take it (and feel pleased with ourselves for the display of honesty.) But what about when the McDonald's "customer service associate" hands us twenty-five cents too much in change? All of a sudden our honesty evaporates because we think it is "too small" and "doesn't matter." But the essence of character is that it operates all of the time and in every situation.

True character operates regardless of the consequences. It is easy to deal honestly with the faults of others. But what about when you are on the hot seat? This is the real test of character. Do you have the integrity to own up to your own mistakes, even when it might mean that you suffer some penalty or disadvantage? Don't let your pride squelch your character.

Is It OK to Laugh?

Does this "all-character, all-of-the-time" approach mean that life will be boring? Absolutely not! We think that people with a strong character can have the best sense of humor. Because they have decided what must be taken absolutely seriously, they are free to take everything else lightly.

Your Faith Makes It All Work

A strong faith in God gives you assurance to stand firm in your convictions regardless of the consequences. When you are trusting God with the circumstances of your life, you don't need to worry about compromising your character in order to maneuver the situation.

Most people take "ethical detours" when they think that they have to strategize or control the outcome of events. When you realize that God is in control, you are relieved of the temptation to violate your principles in order to manipulate the results.

- - - - - - - - - - - - - - - -
What you believe affects the way you think.
The way you think affects the way you live.
- - - - - - - - - - - - - - - -

Living in Truth

The Bible is filled with verses that extol the importance of a strong character. As dads, we can really relate to the following verse in the New Testament:

> I could have no greater joy than to hear that my children live in truth.
>
> 3 JOHN 4

We *suspect* that your parents feel the same way. We *know* that your heavenly Father feels that way.

"Living in truth" means living your life with a Christlike character. That's what the Christian life is all about. God wants us to become like his Son (see Rom 8:29). If you are thinking that such a goal is impossible, you're right: It is (in this lifetime at least). Even the apostle Paul struggled with character issues:

> I know I am rotten through and through so far as my old sinful nature is concerned. No matter which way I turn, I can't make myself do right. I want to, but I can't. When I want to do good, I don't. And when I try not to do wrong, I do it anyway.
>
> ROMANS 7:18-19

Following the Path

We will never achieve perfect Christlike character on this earth. That will only happen when we are united with Christ when he returns (see 1 Jn 3:2). In the meantime, we can follow biblical principles for living in truth.

- *Living in truth begins with **transformed thinking***. Our society doesn't place much value on virtue. We're told that ethics is a private matter and that morality is relative. You could never develop a strong character with a philosophy that says there is nothing worth believing in. The apostle Paul said that living for God requires a complete change in your mindset.

> Don't copy the behavior and customs of this world, but let God transform you into a new person by changing the way you think. Then you will know what God wants you to do, and you will know how good and pleasing and perfect his will really is.
>
> ROMANS 12:2

- *Living in truth is sustained by **consistent conduct***. Our character isn't going to be developed if we only exercise it on Sundays and religious holidays. Character is strengthened over the course of many acts, and it can be severely weakened by repeated compromise. Living in truth requires consistent and persistent focus on those things that are good, right, and true. Here are the apostle Paul's instructions to stay focused and consistent in life:

> And now, dear brothers and sisters, let me say one more thing as I close this letter. Fix your thoughts on what is true and honorable and right. Think about things that are pure and lovely and admirable. Think about things that are excellent and worthy of praise.
>
> PHILIPPIANS 4:8

- *Living in truth realizes God's **present purpose***. You may find it easier to live in truth when you realize that God wants to be active and alive in you right now. He has a present plan and purpose for your life. He isn't intending to put your life "on hold" for a few years until you finish college or get settled in a career. He wants to use you now. This reason alone should give you great motivation to live in truth.

- - - - - - - - - - - - - - -

Your *reputation* can be damaged by the opinion of others. Only you can damage your *character.*

- - - - - - - - - - - - - - -

Your Personal Mission Statement

Maintaining your balance after high school may be your greatest challenge in the next few years. We don't mean that you'll have trouble standing up straight with so many college books in your backpack. We're talking about balance in your life: emotional, mental, physical, and spiritual.

You will be bombarded with new experiences, influences, and opinions. In the whirlwind of your newfound freedom and responsibilities, how can you determine if you are staying balanced and true to your priorities and beliefs? In other words, how can you check to make sure you aren't compromising your character?

In the business world, companies "stay on track" by developing a mission statement—a concise declaration of purpose. It articulates the philosophy of the company as well as describes its product or service. A mission statement explains what the company does in the context of its core values. The mission statement of Delta Air Lines is a good example: *It is the mission of Delta Air Lines to be a Worldwide Airline of Choice.*

Worldwide:	We provide our customers access to the world.
Airline:	We will stay in the business we know best.
Choice:	We want customers to choose us because of the quality of our company, the way we maintain airplanes, the way we fly the airplanes, and the way we serve our customers.

With this mission statement, Delta can easily evaluate its business. The company knows exactly what it wants to do.

Suppose that some entrepreneur presents a great proposal to the CEO of Delta for establishing athletic fitness centers at major airports. Even if this proposal is a surefire money-maker, that executive doesn't need to waste time thinking about it because it doesn't fit within Delta's mission statement. (It has nothing to do with moving people to destinations, and it involves a business that Delta knows nothing about.)

Write Your Own Mission Statement

We have a mission statement for our writing partnership. It reads as follows:

> **It is our passion to present biblical truth in a correct, clear, and casual manner that encourages people to connect in a meaningful way with the living God.**

Writing your own personal mission statement is a good way to keep your character in focus. A personal mission statement is like a personal constitution. Like the U.S. Constitution, your personal mission statement should be:

- *Timeless.* The U.S. Constitution has only been changed twenty-six times during more than two hundred years (and ten of those changes were in the original Bill of Rights). So, too, your personal mission statement should be able to endure over the years. It should state your personal philosophy and beliefs that define your character at any age. Your mission statement will be the expression of your fixed beliefs that apply regardless of any change in your situation or circumstances.

- *Fundamental.* The U.S. Constitution is the standard by which every new law is evaluated. Your personal mission statement can work the same way. Everything that you want to do can by evaluated by whether it falls within the parameters of your mission statement. If it doesn't match up, then you have to analyze why you are doing it.

- *Idealistic.* The U.S. Constitution describes America at its best. As a country, we haven't always lived up to that standard, but our Constitution gives us the benchmark we are always striving for. There will be times when you fall short of the values of your personal mission statement. But don't lower the standards to cover your worst behavior. Instead, set the ideals of your mission statement high enough to raise the level of your thoughts and conduct.

Once you have written your personal mission statement, you have a basis for determining whether any use of your time, energy, and resources is compromising your character. You will have a framework for making sure that the direction and vision for your life is consistent with your character.

A Few of Our Favorites

For the past few semesters, Bruce has been teaching the "Introduction to Leadership" class at Westmont College for first-year students. As an assignment, each student is required to write a personal mission statement. Here are a few of our favorites:

- My mission is to demonstrate Jesus' love and compassion through my life to my family, friends, and peers. To prepare myself, I must focus on Jesus daily through prayer and devotion. I will attempt to do this by serving others with humility.

- I seek to lead a passionate, balanced life in which I accomplish excellence in the eyes of God.

- With integrity and love I will emulate the will of God, walk in the footsteps of Jesus Christ, adhere to the voice of the Holy Spirit, and further the Kingdom of God with passion and reckless abandonment every day of my life.

- I will seek to honor and glorify God by living a life which reflects truth (from studying his Word), integrity (by living his Word), and passion (in communicating his Word).

Learn From Those Around You

One of the best ways to learn about character and to develop your own is to examine the lives of others. Of course, you will find many examples in the pages of the Bible, not the least of which is Christ himself. But you have lots of living examples around you. Sometimes the character of these people inspires us; other times, their lapses in character serve as a warning to us.

Heroes

OK, we want to be very clear about this. We aren't talking about superheroes (the kind on the Underoos you wore as a kid or the kind in comic books, TV shows, or movies). And we certainly aren't talking about celebrities (of either the sports or entertainment variety). We're talking about real-life heroes— people who exemplify our ideals and whose lives exhibit our highest values.

There is nothing wrong with having a hero. It is our heroes who embody the character that we want to have. The best candidates for "hero" status are people who are dead (because a little history has to pass before the person's character is recognized and remembered). Even though these people are far from perfect, they refused to let their frailties prevent them from using their strengths. When we think of them, we should not focus on their imperfections or their accomplishments, but we should admire the traits of their character.

Your heroes might be famous (Abraham Lincoln, Eleanor Roosevelt, George Washington Carver, Amelia Erhart), or they could be obscure (if we could give you an example, then they wouldn't be obscure). Fame is not the important quality of a hero; instead, you are looking at the diligence of the virtuous pursuit in the face of adversity. That type of character is something worth admiring.

Role Models

There is a big difference between heroes and role models:

- *Role models are people you see on a regular basis.* Heroes are admired from a distance (usually because they have been dead for generations).

- *Role models show you how things actually get done.* Heroes inspire you with ideals and concepts.

- *Role models show the techniques.* Heroes are the philosophy.

Both heroes and role models will be helpful in character formation, but you will get the most practical assistance from the role model.

Don't expect to find a role model who is famous. (Famous people probably won't be hanging around where you can see them.) Besides, fame isn't a necessary criteria for a good role model. You are only interested in finding someone who is a few stages ahead of you and who is managing life in a way you admire.

You want a role model who is successful (in terms of the quality of his or her character and life). Maybe this will be a person at your church or a supervisor where you work. Watch what they do, and see how they respond to circumstances. If you are going to college, your role model might be a senior who is doing well academically and is heavily involved in social issues. Perhaps you admire the way this senior is able to keep everything in balance. Don't be afraid to ask a few questions and receive a few practical pointers.

Speaking of practical pointers, when you are looking for a role model, find someone who has a personality and talents that are similar to your own. It won't work if you try to emulate the work habits of a person who is totally different from yourself.

Mentors

A mentor is different from both a hero and a role model. Mentoring involves an advising and counseling relationship with some accountability. A mentor is someone who will commit to be a personal "coach" to you.

Mentors won't seek you out; you must approach them. In fact, beware the person who is too anxious to be your mentor (a kook in search of a groupie). A serious mentoring relationship takes a lot of time, but your mentor will be willing to make such a commitment to you if you show a sincere interest in learning and personal growth. Maybe one of your church leaders or a professor at college would be a good mentor for you.

You Gotta Be You

The bottom line: Your character is between you and God. It cannot be purchased, inherited, or borrowed from someone else. You can get help, advice, instruction, and inspiration from the Bible, your heroes, role models, and mentors, but the responsibility of developing your character belongs entirely to you. Take this job seriously.

Handling Your Free Time

One of the first tests of your character after high school will be how you handle the seemingly unlimited freedom that is available to you. If your character is strong, you can avoid wasting and abusing your free time. If your character is weak, you'll have lots of wasted time and nothing to show for it.

For your entire life through high school, the time frame of your life was fairly rigid. Your daily routine probably went something like this:

- You begin the day by turning off the alarm clock and going back to sleep.
- Next, you hear a parent yelling, "You've overslept! Get out of bed!" You go back to sleep.
- You finally get out of bed, skipping shower and breakfast, and sneak into the first-period class as the sound waves of the tardy bell are dissipating.
- For the next seven hours, you respond to class bells, moving in zombielike fashion between classes.
- After the school dismissal bell, it's a few hours of some job, sport, or activity, according to the schedule imposed by your employer, coach, advisor, or parent.
- You eat a generic dinner before driving to some activity with the church youth group or with friends. You arrive home after curfew (but not so late as to get into *real* trouble with your parents), and you fall asleep after setting the alarm clock for a time earlier than you know you will really get up.

When you think of it this way, your entire life seems controlled by adults and bells.

After high school, all of that changes. Oh, there are still adults and bells around, but they don't control your life unless you allow them to. Your daily routine could go something like this:

- You begin the day by awakening peacefully. No alarm sounded because you didn't set the clock. It is noon. You go back to sleep.
- Next, you awake in time for an afternoon snack while watching a few "Saved by the Bell" reruns.

- A leisurely dinner with friends at Taco Bell is followed by a movie and then a fruit smoothie at the Jamba Juice Joint. You catch Leno and Letterman and fall asleep during Conan.

Now, doesn't this sound much more serene? No stress with this lifestyle—not until you flunk out of school, lose your job, and are evicted from your apartment.

You can know all of the best time-management principles (see Chapter One), but your character must be strong enough to motivate you to use them.

Bruce & Stan's Ethics Check

Do you think all of this talk about character is irrelevant to your everyday life? Well, think again. If fact, as we close this chapter, we give you three questions that are sure to arise in your "real life after high school" world. These are little, seemingly innocuous circumstances. See whether you think character plays a role in how you would respond in each of these situations.

1. If the restaurant has free refills, should you save money by purchasing just one drink for two or more people?

2. Since it doesn't cost the cable company any extra, should you save money by wiring your apartment for cable off your neighbor's box?

3. Should you download copyrighted software programs from a friend's computer, since the program has already been paid for *once*?

Moving On

Now that we have talked about character, let's move to the subject that will likely be the greatest challenge to your character or the greatest help to it: your friends.

As you already know from personal experience, some of your friends encourage you to live a life that is consistent with your character; other friends may pressure you to compromise your character. As we'll discuss in the next chapter, the choice is up to you. Choose wisely.

CHAPTER 5

Friends—Choose or Lose

As much as you'd like to think that you are ready to become the person you want to be—in the place you're going to spend the next few years, with your personal character and integrity completely intact—there's still one missing ingredient to your life: *people.*

We don't mean just *any* people—like your roommate or the people down the hall or your parents or your professors or your employers. These are the people you're stuck with, for better or for worse. (C'mon, it's not that bad.) We're talking about people who are much more fun, much more special, and much more influential. We're talking about your *friends.*

Ah, friends. They're probably a very important part of your life right now. Your friends have always been there for you. They basically got you through high school. Unlike your family, who wants to change you, your friends accept you for who you are, just the way you are. They don't judge you. No wonder the wisest man who ever lived said, "A real friend sticks closer than a brother" (Prv 18:24).

It's Time

Now, we'd love to sing the praises of your wonderful friends for the rest of this chapter, but before we go any further, we feel it is our duty to help you face up to a harsh reality. This isn't going to be easy for us to say, but someone has to be honest with you, and it may as well be us. So here goes:

You need to get some new friends.

Ouch! That was cold (sorry). But before you slam this book shut, allow us to explain what we mean. We think you'll find there's a method to our madness.

Friends are such a powerful force in your life—and you in theirs—that you can no longer afford to just "let it happen." Let's face it, if you're like most people, you haven't used as much discretion as you should have in your choice of friends (hey, we've all been there). Among your friends you probably have at least one:

- *Preppie:* There's nothing wrong with dressing in style, but these people sometimes use fashion and style to judge and exclude others.
- *Partier:* The person who lives for parties and drinking and not much else.
- *Stoner:* A drug user.
- *Racist:* You know this person's jokes and comments are out of line. *Way* out of line.
- *Loser:* A negative influence who doesn't do anything well except bring you down.

We're not saying these people have no value. They just have no value *as friends.* Yes, it's true that God could use you to influence them for good (except for the Preppie, who is beyond help). But our guess is that if you haven't had any influence by now, it's not going to happen any time soon.

Now is your chance to make a break from these people, even if you've known them since the third grade (chances are they won't miss you).

The Value of Friendship

Whether you are staying home for a while after high school or moving away to go to college or for some other reason, the friendships you make over the next few years will be invaluable as you prepare for your future and fulfill your purpose.

If you choose your friends wisely, they will become an important source of encouragement and inspiration. No longer do you have to put up with friends who tear you down by their bad example or negative attitudes. You have the power to become friends with people who will challenge and motivate you and push you to be a better person.

- - - - - - - - - - - - - - - - -
WARNING: As you venture out on your own, there will be times when loneliness will set in. Count on it.
- - - - - - - - - - - - - - - - -

One day you may find yourself hungry for your mother's liver pudding or even wishing that you could see your pesky little brother. Even though you are surrounded by roommates or even casual acquaintances, you can still have a need for true friends who will comfort you and pray for you.

That's another good reason to find new friends, especially if your old friends are many miles away. Yes, you can "reach out and touch someone" through the phone or E-mail, but there's nothing like a friend who's near.

Friends Are Only Human

We don't have to tell you that friends can and will let you down. Even a friend you completely trust—perhaps a friend you look up to as a mentor or role model—is capable of bringing you great disappointment. Why? Because, like you and like us, friends are fallible human beings.

Always give a friend the benefit of the doubt.

When a friend lets you down or, even worse, betrays you, it's critical to confront the situation as soon as you can. Don't let your feelings fester. For one thing, festering is never healthy; for another, you could be wrong about your friend. "A friend is always loyal" (Prv 17:17). Refuse to believe rumors about your friends, and never spread them. Go to your friend and ask for the truth.

The same thing applies if you have been personally offended by something your friend has said or done. Again, it may be a total misunderstanding, or your friend may have really blown it. Either way, you need to go to your friend first before talking to other people about it.

Knowing in advance that your friend will let you down should not deter you from making friends. Don't be like the cynic who says, "It's not that I'm against humanity; it's people I can't stand." You need friends. You just have to be wise about how you choose them. To get you started, we want to give you a few tips on how to form friendships. We're going to start with the most important friend you'll ever have and work our way down from there.

The Greatest Friend in the World

There are several criteria you could use to choose friends. In fact, we're going to ask you to place the following qualities of friendship in order of importance:

__ has a cool car

__ gives you lecture notes when you don't go to class

__ has your best interest in mind all the time

__ buys beer for you

__ forgives you no matter what you have done

__ loans you that cool car

__ loans you money

__ knows you better than anyone else

How does your list look? What are the top qualities you would look for in a friend? Wouldn't it be great to have a friend who knows you better than anyone else? Well, guess what? You already do. His name is God.

Now, you may not believe us, because you probably think God has a lot more important things to do than be your friend (like run the universe). Yes, God is very involved in our world, but his first priority is you. You don't have to just take our word for it. Here's what the Bible says about God knowing you:

Not even a sparrow, worth only half a penny, can fall to the ground without your Father knowing it. And the very hairs on your head are all numbered. So don't be afraid; you are more valuable to him than a whole flock of sparrows.

MATTHEW 10:29-31

This isn't fairy tale stuff. The God who knows everything (it's called *omniscience*) and can do anything (that's called *omnipotence*) knows *you* completely. And here's the kicker: even though he knows everything about you, he still loves you unconditionally. "This is real love. It is not that we loved God, but that he loved us" (1 Jn 4:10).

Jesus Is the Key

Do you remember singing this song as a youngster in church:
"Yes, Jesus loves me. Yes, Jesus loves me.
"Yes, Jesus loves me. The Bible tells me so."

What the Bible *tells* you is that "God so loved the world that he gave his only Son, so that everyone who believes in him will not perish but have eternal life" (Jn 3:16). Jesus, the Son of God, is the one who makes it possible for us to be God's friend:

"So now we can rejoice in our wonderful new relationship with God—all because of what our Lord Jesus Christ has done for us in making us friends of God" (Rom 5:11).

Make Friends With Your Family

So far in this book we've talked a lot about leaving home. Even if you aren't leaving home in a physical sense, you are in the process of leaving as you take on more responsibility for yourself. You will always be a part of your family and your heritage. You can never truly leave your family, no matter how much you'd like to at times.

Even though it might seem as though your family wants to run your life, you need to embrace your family as your friends. We've put this category of friendship right below God in importance because no other earthly friendships will be more important to you. This includes your parents, your grandparents, your siblings, your uncles and aunts, and your cousins. If and when you get married, your spouse, your children, and eventually your grandchildren will become your best friends.

Perhaps you don't feel this way about your family. At this stage in your life, your friends may mean more to you than your family. Believe us when we say that your friends will come and go, but your family will always be there. Blood really is thicker than water.

What If Your Family Is Dysfunctional, Abusive, or Irresponsible?

You may come from a family with real problems. We aren't experts in the field of dysfunctional families; if you need help to figure out how to handle your particular family situation, your pastor or priest may be able to direct you to someone who can help.

There is one thing we can tell you for sure, however. There is a way to overcome your family challenges, and it's not going to come from trying to change them. The greatest thing you can do is to love your family members where they are and pray for them every day.

Our good friend and mentor, John Trent, has written about his relationship with his father, which was difficult for as long as he knew his father. John never stopped loving his dad, even on his father's deathbed, where his father still refused to give John his approval. John never let his father's dysfunction stand in the way of his own success and responsibility before God, but he also never stopped loving and respecting his father.

Your Pastor Is a Friend Who Guides You

We all need spiritual leaders in our lives, people ordained by God to watch over us and to pray for us. If you have never made friends with your pastor or priest, you are missing out on an incredibly rich friendship. If you've never been in the habit of going to church, now would be a great time to start (more about church in Chapter Eleven).

Especially if you are away from home, you need the stability and account-ability of a church. You need to be around people who care about your spiritual needs. When you find a church, introduce yourself to the pastor. If the church is very large, you should get to know the associate pastor or the college pastor. Tell your pastor that you want to form a friendship. "Remember your leaders who first taught you the word of God. Think of all the good that has come from their lives, and trust the Lord as they do" (Heb 13:7).

How to Learn About Mentors

If you are interested in learning more about what it takes to establish or build a mentor relationship, we recommend the book *Mentoring: Confidence in Finding a Mentor and Becoming One* by Bobb Biehl, II. Also, read any book by or about Helen Keller, the famous woman who was both blind and deaf, but who overcame her physical limitations to become an international activist for handicapped people. Her success was due largely to her lifelong mentor, Anne Sullivan. The story of Sullivan and Keller's mentor-student relationship is a classic for the ages.

Your Mentor Is a Friend Who Teaches You

We touched upon mentors in the previous chapter. A mentor is a teacher chosen by you to offer guidance and advice. People who don't seek out mentors miss out on a rich and rewarding source of friendship.

All great achievers have mentors. Sometimes they're called coaches or teachers. The key is that you want to learn and you're willing to submit to someone who agrees to teach you.

Find Friends Who Are Friends With God

After God, your family, your pastor, and your mentor, the most important friends you can have are friends who are friends with God.

We're not saying you should never make friends with people who aren't Christians. To the contrary, as a Christian, part of your mission in the world is to make friends with people who don't know God personally. We're just saying that you should make it a priority to seek out Christian friends first. Before you can hope to be a positive influence to others, you need people around you who will be a positive influence to you.

We admit that finding these kinds of friends may not be as easy as it sounds. How do you find quality friends? Where do you look? What do you look for?

Finding "Forever Friends"

Here's the best formula we know of for finding long-lasting friendship:

<blockquote>
To find good friends,
you need to be a good friend.
</blockquote>

You can't necessarily pick your friends and then expect them to fall in line, willing to be your friend. It's a lot more effective to *be* the kind of friend you are looking for to others.

In his classic book, *The Friendship Factor*, Dr. Alan Loy McGinnis lists these five ways to deepen your relationships:[1]

1. "Assign top priority to your relationships." Don't be a "fair-weather friend" or a part-time friend. It's better to be a good friend to a few people than a lousy friend to many.
2. "Cultivate transparency." There isn't one personality trait that defines a good friend, but there is one quality that does: *openness*. If you

aren't willing to be open and honest with your friends, then you aren't really a friend.

3. "Dare to talk about your affection." By "affection" Dr. McGinnis means "warmth" more than physical expression. A true friend is a caring friend.

4. "Learn the gestures of love." Demonstrate consideration, kindness, and giving, which should take place in a true friendship as well as in a marriage relationship.

5. "Create space in your relationship." Dr. McGinnis writes that the tendency to control others "gets the prize for ruining more relationships than any other." If you want to be a good friend, give your friends room. Jealousy is a nasty trait in any relationship.

Finding Quality Friends

OK, finally we've arrived at the category of friendship you're most familiar and comfortable with—people like you. Ordinary people without titles or offices. These are the people you're likely to see every day, that you'll *want* to see every day. These are your friends.

As we've been saying, now is your chance to build some new friendships with quality people. The best advice we found on this subject comes from *The Campus Connection,* a book written by seven experienced campus ministers. Here is a summary of the principles they share for finding quality friends:[2]

1. The best friendships happen without a lot of work.

2. Share your values, including your faith.

3. Ask yourself, "Will this person help me grow (spiritually, emotionally, intellectually)?"

4. Ask yourself, "What can I contribute to the relationship?"

5. Ask yourself, "Can I be myself around this person and be accepted?"

Places to Meet Quality Friends

We recommend the following places where you are more likely to meet quality friends: *church, service clubs, spiritual retreats, cafes, and concerts (preferably jazz, contemporary Christian, or classical).*

Here are some places less likely to yield quality friendships: *bars, dance clubs, meetings of the Aryan Nation, and concerts (where the musicians perform naked or sing about Satan).*

What to Do About "Negative Influences"

There's a chance that, as you've been reading this book, you realize that you've already made some poor choices in friends. You may have even broken off some lousy friendships from high school, but you're already back under the negative influence of some new friends.

First of all, the fact that you're thinking about your poor choices is a good thing. Maybe you will be less likely to repeat your mistakes in the future. For now—and the sooner you do this the better—here's what to do:

• Avoid the friends that have a negative influence on you (as we said before, they won't miss you).

• Don't abandon a good friend going bad. Confront him or her in a loving way.

• If your words have no effect, be willing to cut the ties but continue to pray for your friend.

What About Fraternities and Sororities?

We have to admit that neither of us has any experience with the Greeks on campus (geeks, yes; Greeks, no). So we can only tell you what we've heard and read.

Fraternities and sororities are a time-honored tradition at North American colleges and universities. Many a successful person can trace his or her strength as a student and later as a graduate to a fraternity or sorority. We're told that fraternity brothers and sorority sisters make friends for life.

That doesn't mean that you have to join a Greek club if you want lifelong friends and valuable business contacts. We're just pointing out one of the benefits often cited by Greek advocates.

On the negative side, fraternities and sororities seem to receive more than their share of publicity over the problem of drinking. Truthfully, the connection between college students and alcohol goes way beyond fraternities and sororities. The problem on campuses is so acute that many colleges and universities are finally waking up and taking steps to curb drinking, especially the deadly practice of "binge" drinking.

The question you have to ask yourself is this: Is it wise to put yourself in a position where you will be continuously exposed to alcohol (or drugs or tobacco), which will not only damage your body but could impair your relationships with others, including God? Or would it be better to live in an environment that encourages you to do the right thing, whether it's in the spiritual, moral, or intellectual part of your life?

Yes, There Are Christian Fraternities and Sororities

If you just have to be a Greek, check out one of the many Christian Greek houses located around the country. One of the oldest and best-known fraternities is Alpha Gamma Omega, a national Christ-centered organization. Founded on the campus of UCLA in 1927, Alpha Gamma Omega has chapters on several college campuses (their Web site is www.ago.org). Their motto: *Fraternity for Eternity.*

Influencing Others

Here's an exciting thought for you as you enter your career as a college student:

Wherever you are, God wants to use you to influence others.

The last message Jesus gave to us was that, as his followers, we are to "go into all the world and preach the Good News to everyone, everywhere" (Mk 16:15). You see, as a Christ-follower, your job is to be a witness for Christ wherever you are in the world. Right now, whether you're in college or working in a job or both, Christ is asking you to tell others about him.

This is what we mean by your "mission to the world." Yes, you need to build your friendship network by first finding friends who share your values. But don't isolate yourself in a "Christian comfort zone" (this is especially true if you are at a Christian college). Follow the example of Christ, who called himself "a friend of the worst sort of sinners" (Lk 7:34).

- - - - - - - - - - - - - - - - -

Don't make friends with people in order to share or endorse their lifestyle. Rather, make friends in order to influence them for Christ.

- - - - - - - - - - - - - - - - -

Like the apostle Paul, you and your Christian friends should see yourselves as "Christ's ambassadors," believing that God is using you to speak to your non-Christian friends (2 Cor 5:20). Whether you are dealing with your roommate, a professor, a fraternity brother or sorority sister, a coworker, or a new friend in class, you need to know that you may be the best ambassador for Christ that person has ever encountered. And just so you won't feel any unnecessary pressure, you need to also know that it is "Christ in you"— not you—that will draw others to Christ. Because you are willing to be used by God, your life will be "a fragrance presented by Christ to God" (2 Cor 2:15).

Because you are Christ's ambassador, you will inevitably get questions from your non-Christian friends—questions related to God and the peace of heart and mind you radiate. Don't be *afraid* of these questions. Be *ready* to answer them:

> And if you are asked about your Christian hope, always be ready to explain it. But you must do this in a gentle and respectful way.
>
> 1 PETER 3:15-16

Being ready to answer questions about your faith and God means doing some study. Read the Bible daily, and also read books that will help you explain your faith. We like *Bruce & Stan's Guide to God* (yes, we wrote it) and Josh McDowell's *A Ready Defense*.

Radical Lifestyles

During your college years it is a virtual certainty that you will encounter an array of lifestyles unlike anything you have ever seen (notice we said "encounter" rather than "experience"). But here's the amazing part. If you are a Christian in a secular college, intent on living out your faith, *you* are going to be the one pegged as *radical*. Your lifestyle of living for Christ is going to be an affront and will appear "foolish" to those living in darkness. But don't despair and don't condemn. Instead, draw strength from the wisdom of Paul in the Bible:

"I know very well how foolish the message of the cross sounds to those who are on the road to destruction. But we who are being saved recognize this message as the very power of God" (1 Cor 1:18).

Befriending the Friendless

Wherever you go throughout your life, you're going to meet the friendless. These are the outcasts, the oddballs, the strange. When high-school students cruelly exclude and ridicule these outcasts, we can partially explain their behavior as being ignorant or misguided. But as a full-fledged adult, you have no such excuse. If you deliberately contribute to the exclusion of another human being from your little group of friends for no other reason than that he or she is "different," shame on you.

Instead of excluding, try including the loner, the unlovely, and the unusual person. Don't force it, but do your best to uncover the inner beauty and intrinsic value of that person. Become a friend to the friendless.

Home for the Holidays

There will come a time during your first few months away from home that you will return home—probably for Thanksgiving or Christmas. This is a grand occasion for three reasons:

1. You'll get some home cooking for a change.

2. Everybody will be glad to see you.

3. You'll have an opportunity to show your family and old friends how much you have changed—for the better.

The easiest thing in the world would be to pick up where you left off by running with the same old friends and slipping back into your old habits. But that would also be a big mistake. It's not that you're suddenly better than everyone back home. You don't want to give the people you know the impression that "the fancy college boy is too good for us now."

Pray and ask God to give you a humble and grateful spirit as you go home. Stand firm in your conviction and your new pattern of associating with quality friends, but still show consideration and love to any of your old friends who happen to seek you out. And if by chance someone asks you, "What happened? You seem different," be ready to give an answer that just might change that person's life.

Moving On

We could go on and on about friends and friendships—as a matter of fact, we will! In the next chapter we're going to talk about friendships that go beyond casual to something more meaningful and challenging.

Jennifer B., age 21

CHAPTER 6

More Than Friends—
Dating and Beyond

When it comes to friendships, the sky is the limit. The various combinations of guys and girls and ages and interests are almost limitless. With casual friendships you still have options. You don't *have* to see all your friends every day. You don't even have to call or E-mail them. If you need to retreat into solitude, you can and nobody will bother you (of course, if you retreat for too long, you would hope that at least one of your friends would call to see if you're OK). If you want to go out in a huge group, you can. If you want to hang with two or three friends, no problem. The only obligation you have is to be a good friend.

However, there may very well come a point when you're ready, willing, and able to develop a deeper friendship with one particular person (and we're not talking roommates here). Specifically, we're referring to guy-girl (or, if you prefer, man-woman) relationships, the kind that go beyond casual friend-ships to deeper human connections.

That Guy-Girl Thing

Romantic relationships can start with a casual friendship, but at some point they move along to the level where a mutual attraction begins to awaken your physical and emotional senses. (Note: Usually the physical "awakening" takes place more quickly in guys, which is why, since the beginning of time, girls have learned to filter out male ogling, drooling, posing, and mindless ban-tering.)

It's almost a sure thing that sometime in your post–high school career you and a member of the opposite sex will find each other attractive. It will be hard to explain because it will involve a combination of your physical, mental, emotional, and spiritual dimensions. This may not be new for you; you probably experienced this attraction in high school.

But now that you're on your own, with all the privileges and rights there-in, you'll want to treat this guy-girl thing with more respect and responsibil-ity. In fact, we have a little theory about this guy-girl thing. Try this on for size (by the way, feel free to apply our theory to situations other than rela-tionships, such as scuba diving and surgery):

The deeper you go, the more responsible you must become.

You're probably going to have more than one serious relationship over the next few years, and you may end up in a relationship with someone you are convinced is "the one." The key is that, in each relationship, you need to show respect and practice responsibility. And the more serious you get in each relationship, the more responsible you must become.

If you're not willing to be responsible, then you shouldn't get serious. Going deeper in any relationship without responsibility shows no respect for the other person or for yourself. And ultimately you show no respect for God.

Are You Leaving Someone Behind?

If you're leaving home, you could be leaving someone special behind. Or the two of you may be taking different paths as you enter your college years. Either way, how do you break things up gracefully ... or should you break up at all?

We know a young man who just graduated from high school and left home for college. He had a sweet girlfriend in his hometown who was still in high school. We were very impressed with how this guy handled this difficult situation. Because God was at the center of their relationship while they were dating, he kept God at the center when they broke up. Why did they break up at all? He felt it was important for each of them to meet new people and experience new things. Taking the lead, this young man prayed with his girlfriend, committing their futures to God. Though parting was difficult, they both knew they were doing the right thing.

At last report, the young man is enjoying his college experience very much, and his former girlfriend is successfully finishing high school.

On the other hand, we have known Christian couples who went off to different schools (in some cases they agreed to see other people, in other cases not) only to wind up together. Pray about what God has in store for you, both individually and as a couple, and be open to the direction in which God is leading you both.

Love is patient and kind. Love is not jealous or boastful or proud or rude. Love does not demand its own way. Love is not irritable, and it keeps no record of when it has been wronged. It is never glad about injustice but rejoices whenever the truth wins out. Love never gives up, never loses faith, is always hopeful, and endures through every circumstance.

1 CORINTHIANS 13:4-7

Free and Easy

Since you're in a new environment, you can be who you want to be. You can act how you want to act, especially around other people. Great! Go for it. But keep your head. Whether you're hanging out with friends or seeing one particular person, it's always a good idea to root your free spirit in respect for others and responsibility before God.

R.E.S.P.E.C.T.

OK, we've *talked* enough about respect. It's time to give you our personal philosophy on what it means to respect others, especially others of the opposite sex, and particularly the special people with whom you decide to develop a deeper relationship. Here's our take on respect:

R: *Relationships matter.* The way you relate to others determines your success in life.

E: *Everything counts.* There are no trivial relationships, and nothing in your relationships is trivial.

S: *Show respect.* Every person is someone's son or daughter; more important, every person is someone God loves.

P: *Pray for guidance.* God cares about you and the people you know. Ask him for help.

E: *Expect God's best.* Don't settle for second best. Expect God to lead you to quality relationships, and remember that God expects your best as well.

C: *Charity (love) is best.* Love is more than a feeling. Love is wanting the best for the other person.

T: *Trust God.* Be patient and believe that God will guide you each step of the way.

You see how this works? Nobody expects you to carry note cards with you listing Bruce & Stan's philosophy of respect. But we guarantee that if you follow the principles, you will enjoy your relationships more, others will enjoy and respect you more, and you will never lose your self-respect.

- - - - - - - - - - - - - - - -
The Bottom Line:
Respect is the foundation of any relationship, especially a dating relationship.
- - - - - - - - - - - - - - - -

Dating 201

You were probably wondering when we were going to mention the magic word: *dating*. Now that we have, let's talk about what we mean.

In case you hadn't noticed, the concept of dating has gone through a revolution of sorts. A lot of people have tried to redefine dating, while others have avoided the subject altogether. We're not going to take that position. We're going to deal with dating head-on because we happen to think it's a very good idea.

Hey, we still date! (We date our wives, of course. We recommend that every married couple continue to date one another.) You might be surprised to know that the dictionary still defines *dating* as "the practice or an instance of having social engagements with a person of the opposite sex." Sounds pretty harmless, doesn't it? Harmless yet important.

Now that you're at the college level, you're ready to move up in your dating courses. In high school you took Dating 101, an introductory class. Here you learned—through trial and error—the rudiments of being with a guy or girl on a date. What kind of grade did you get in Dating 101? If you got a C or better, you're ready to move on. If you failed, or if you never took the class at all, we're going to promote you anyway. We don't want you to get any further behind.

Kiss Dating ... Hello?
A few years ago a best-selling book encouraged singles to "kiss dating good-bye." The author contended that, since it's very difficult to practice dating while remaining physically, emotionally, and spiritually pure, it's best to avoid dating altogether until you're ready to make a commitment to one person for life in a marriage relationship.

We agree that it's important to put God first in every aspect of life, including every relationship we cultivate. However, we also think that to avoid dating altogether is a bit extreme. It puts undue pressure on those who are in dating relationships to make a marriage commitment before they are ready—emotionally, financially, or experientially.

When done responsibly, dating can make you a better person. Dating helps you relate to the opposite sex (which you'll have to do all your life, even if you never get married). Here are some other reasons.

Why Date?

Our being old enough to be your parents has its advantages when it comes to this topic of dating. For one thing, we've done a lot of dating (we got to know our wives on dates before we married them, and we continue to date because we continue to enjoy our "social engagements"). In addition, we have been able to observe our own kids through the high school and college years as they have dated.

Because of this "dating experience," both as participants and observers, we have seen several benefits to dating:

- Dating civilizes you.
- Dating develops your social skills.
- Dating teaches you how to live on a budget.
- Dating shows you how the opposite sex thinks and feels.
- Dating helps you determine the kinds of qualities you enjoy in another person.

Dating doesn't have to be the prelude to anything more, but we think dating is a necessary prerequisite to growing deeper in an honest and honorable relationship with someone of the opposite sex. As long as you remember the R.E.S.P.E.C.T. principles, you can cultivate valuable and special friendships without worrying about the pressure of permanent commitment. When you are ready to commit yourself in marriage, you will have already learned a lot about understanding and caring for your future husband or wife.

A Balanced Approach to Dating

By now we hope you've noticed a definite theme running through this book (and frankly, we hope it's a theme that runs through your life). The theme is *balance*. Whether we're talking about

- becoming the person God wants you to be,
- choosing the best friends possible,
- maintaining a healthy lifestyle,
- keeping your finances in order,
- selecting a career that's best for you, or
- entering the world of dating,

one of the important keys to your success is *balance*.

We're not talking *boring mediocrity* here. Ask professional people—athletes, musicians, entertainers, scientists, businesspeople—and you'll hear the same advice. If you keep a balanced perspective, seeking the best in all areas, maintaining a solid position, learning from the successes (and mistakes) of others, you will succeed yourself ... and have fun doing it.

When it comes to dating, balance means you don't get caught up in a dating frenzy, where you're running ragged or where you're putting yourself in potentially compromising positions (and we think you know what we mean). But neither are you isolating yourself in your room or hiding behind the dynamics of a group, afraid to get close to anyone. Yes, you may have been hurt in the past, and the last thing you want is another relationship. Maybe you're so busy that the last thing you have time for is dating. Maybe you want to date, but nobody's asking or everyone you ask turns you down.

Be patient. The right person will come along, if not for life, then for your next date! In the meantime, take the pressure off yourself. Enjoy your friends and relax. But don't stop reading. The dating tips ahead will come in handy someday (and maybe sooner than you think). And if you're heading out the door for a date in the next thirty minutes, read fast. The next few paragraphs will help keep you balanced.

Treat Every Date With Respect

You never know. The next person you date may turn out to be your spouse (don't let that scare you). It's true! At some point you're going to meet for the first time the person you're going to marry someday. Or if that isn't the case, then your date is likely to become someone else's husband or wife someday. So treat every date with respect. See him or her as God's choice for someone (and that someone could be you) or as someone who will eventually choose to remain purely single.

Something to Think About

You're at the age when many of us meet our lifetime marriage partner. So it's a good idea to avoid getting into a long-term relationship with anyone who

- isn't your type,
- isn't good for you,
- doesn't share your values, or
- doesn't want to get married.

Are You Compatible?

Sounds like a Catch-22. You don't want to date someone seriously with whom you're not compatible. But how can you tell whether you're compatible without dating that person?

Well, we can't help you identify specific personality characteristics ahead of time (that's one of the benefits of dating, to bring out the annoying or endearing habits in the other person). But before you can tell whether you are compatible with someone else, you need to know a few things about *yourself*. You should be able to answer "yes" to these three questions before you even begin dating someone:

Do you know yourself? (See Chapter One.)

Do you know God? (See Chapter Five.)

Does the person you want to date know God? (See 2 Cor 6:14.)

Take It Slowly ...

When it comes to developing deeper relationships, you will never regret taking your time. What you will regret is rushing into something that quickly turns out to be a mismatch. What you may find is that you relate to someone on a superficial level (read: physical), but then you discover over time that in the areas that really matter—spiritual depth, emotional stability, basic personality—you really aren't compatible at all.

Taking it slowly means that you meet somewhere for coffee or Coke and get to know each other before going out on an official date. It means going out in a group before going out alone. It means that after you get to know your new special someone a little, you evaluate whether or not you are truly compatible in the areas that matter. If there's any point where either you or your special friend possesses qualities the other would find intolerable, you need to have the courage and the character to prevent your relationship from moving beyond friendship.

... But Don't Take Too Long!

Now we get to the flip side of this whole relationship process, and that's *commitment* (at this point all the guys reading this book are cringing, while the girls are saying, "Yesss!").

The opposite of rushing into a relationship—especially a marriage relationship—is never wanting to commit. This seems to be a pretty big problem right now, especially among men. There are a variety of reasons for this growing reluctance to commit to one person, especially when that commitment inevitably leads to marriage.

- *You may be from a broken home.* You see marriage as a battleground to be avoided at all costs, not a blessed union of souls.
- *You may be fearful of the financial uncertainty* that lies ahead in the world, not to mention your own bank account. You're still paying off student loans ... from junior high school.
- *You're concentrating on your career.* You are on a course of study that's going to take a while, and after that it's going to take some time to establish your career.

- *You love "playing the field."* Why settle down with one person when that one person will only "tie you down"?
- *You're afraid of intimacy.* You just can't see yourself totally open and honest with another person.

We're not saying these are bad reasons for avoiding commitment, although for your own well-being you may want to talk to someone who can help you work through these issues. You just need to be aware of them and face up to the fact that any one of these reasons may be preventing you from entering into one of the most satisfying and enriching experiences available to mere mortals (you can tell we're biased).

Dating can and should be fun, especially right now. Don't put any unnecessary pressure on yourself, and don't put any pressure on the person you're dating. Nothing kills a relationship more quickly than one of you seeming too eager to get married. Be thoughtful and deliberate about dating, but enjoy the experience as you let it take its natural course. If God has placed in your heart a desire to get married, then rest in the confidence that dating is the best way to discover the person you will eventually fall in love with and marry.

On the other hand, if you've been dating as an adult for many years now, and dating is just a game to you, and you have no intention of ever committing to one person, then we have a little thoughtful advice. Believe us, we're not trying to push you into marriage or even a deeper commitment. But we don't want you to squander your life in a series of unfulfilling relationships just because you are unwilling to make a commitment. Worse, we don't want you to squander someone else's life!

So, if you want it, here's our advice:

- *Grow up.* You're not in high school anymore.
- *Pray hard.* You can't do it alone.
- *Read on.* Get into God's Word. It's amazing what you'll find.
- *Be open.* God will lead you when you least expect it.
- *Be discerning.* Follow your heart, but use your head.
- *Nobody's perfect.* Love looks at the *real* person.
- *Don't settle.* Nothing good happens when you're desperate.

Sexual Purity: It's Your Choice

We get a lot of E-mail from our readers (and we'd love to get one from you—see the introduction for our address). Recently we heard from a young lady who is a new Christian. She told us that her boyfriend, who encouraged her to become a Christian, was upset when she told him, "No more sex!" He reasoned that they could be Christians and love each other and have sex. She was torn and confused. Here's what we advised.

Dear Torn and Confused,

The Bible is very clear that sex outside of marriage is wrong. No way around that one. Check out Proverbs 6:32 and 1 Corinthians 6:18. It's not that God doesn't want us to enjoy sex. But he created sex to be a sacred and very personal expression of love between a husband and wife. Anything outside of that is not only wrong but destructive. This may sound "old fashioned," but you don't have to think very much to realize that nothing good—aside from temporary physical pleasure—comes from sex outside of marriage.

It's interesting that your boyfriend is the one who encouraged you to become a Christian, and yet he is upset that you won't have sex with him anymore. Doesn't it make you wonder about his love and respect for you? Take God out of the picture for a minute (your boyfriend has). If his main objective in having a relationship with you is sex, then you don't have much of a relationship. And please don't fall for the old line, "If you really love me, you'll have sex with me." If he really loves you, he'll respect you and honor you rather than seeing you as a physical object to meet his own selfish and misdirected desires.

Your salvation isn't based on what you have done or on what you will do. It's based on the love and work of Jesus Christ on your behalf (Eph 2:8-10). But as you grow in Christ, you are going to find that you will want to please him in all you do. That doesn't mean you won't fail. We all do. But there is a way out. It's not in our own abilities but in Christ's. Only Jesus Christ can get you through this. Pray that he will give you strength and wisdom and courage.

Finding the Love of Your Life

Just because you're serious about commitment doesn't always mean you're ready for it now (remember, take it slowly). What it means is that you choose to enter into the whole process with careful thought, consistent prayer, and all the help you can find.

One of the best places to look for help is in books. It's OK to talk to your friends, but if that's your only source of information, you're in trouble. You're going to get a lot of varying opinions, many of them wrong. Friendly advice is fine, but there's nothing like *sound* advice, the kind found in reliable books.

We're going to recommend two books. The first is *Finding the Love of Your Life* by Dr. Neil Clark Warren.[1] This valuable book contains ten principles for choosing the right marriage partner. For example, under Principle #3, "Find a Person to Love Who Is a Lot Like You," Dr. Warren lists the following similarities that are "absolutely essential" for you to have in common with another person if you want marital happiness:

- Intelligence
- Values
- Intimacy
- Interests
- Expectations

And then there are those "Differences That Spell Trouble." These are the differences between two people that are very difficult to overcome, especially in a marriage:

- Energy level
- Personal habits
- Use of money
- Verbal skills and interests

Whether you're thinking about marriage or not, the other book we think you will find very helpful is Dr. James Dobson's *Life on the Edge*. In it he lists five "straightforward recommendations" you should take to heart.[2]

1. A Sunday School teacher gave Dr. Dobson this advice when he was only thirteen: "Don't marry the person you think you can live with. Marry the one you can't live without."

2. "Don't marry someone who has characteristics that you feel are intolerable." If you can't stand something about the other person now, it's likely you won't see any change in the future.

3. "Do not marry impulsively!" Get to know the person you intend to marry well.

4. "If you are a deeply committed Christian, do not allow yourself to become 'unequally yoked' with an unbeliever." Don't count on converting your spouse once you're married.

5. "Do not move in with a person before marriage." Not only is it wrong before God, but "it undermines a relationship and often leads to divorce."

Marriage Is for Keeps

If you're afraid of the prospect of marriage being a permanent proposition, you should be! But don't be afraid in a negative way that keeps you from ever making a commitment. Be fearful in a positive way (yes, that's possible). In the natural world, fear prevents us from doing things that harm us. The same thing goes for the spiritual world, and marriage is at its core deeply spiritual.

Marriage is an institution established by God for our benefit and his glory. Here's what Jesus said about marriage:

> God's plan was seen from the beginning of creation, for "He made them male and female." "This explains why a man leaves his father and mother and is joined to his wife, and the two are united into one." Since they are no longer two but one, let no one separate them, for God has joined them together.
>
> MARK 10:6-9

So where does the positive fear come in? We need to fear God. Our friend Chuck Swindoll once defined "Fear God" like this: *Take him seriously and do what he says.* There's no question God is serious about marriage. We need to do what God says and treat marriage as his sacred gift to us, a gift he doesn't want returned.

So What About Divorce?

You can't beat around the bush. Divorce is "not what God originally intended" (Mt 19:8). But divorce happens. We are sinners, and things don't always turn out the way we want them to, despite our best intentions.

Without going into a whole discussion as to if and when divorce is necessary, we just want to tell you from experience that it's absolutely vital that you commit to marriage with the idea that it is an "until death do you part" deal. Don't enter into marriage with the idea that divorce is your escape clause. Commit yourself fully to your spouse by committing yourself to God.

Purely Single

> So the person who marries does well, and the person who doesn't marry does even better.
>
> 1 CORINTHIANS 7:38

Those rather surprising words by the apostle Paul were written for a reason. Marriage is a wonderful, sacred thing, but if you want to serve God wholeheartedly with fewer distractions, it's even better to remain single and celibate.

Celibate?

Celibate – 1. A person who takes a vow not to marry: Monks and nuns are celibate. 2. An unmarried person. 3. A person who is abstinent in sexual matters.

Paul is speaking to men here, but you can apply it to women as well. The married person has to think about his or her spouse, so his or her "interests are divided." Paul isn't saying that married people settle for second best. His point is that single people can aspire to something better because of the extra time they can spend serving God.

Bruce & Stan's Top Ten Best Things About Being Single

10. You can wear your "holey underwear" until the elastic breaks.
 9. No pressure to clean the house.
 8. No one cares if you drink out of the milk carton.
 7. You can stay out as long as you want.
 6. You have freedom to take time off for short-term missions.
 5. Only one set of family holiday dinners to deal with.
 4. All the hair in the bathroom is yours.
 3. When you put on your favorite shirt, no one asks, "Are you going to wear that?"
 2. You have extra time to volunteer for community service projects.
 1. You can spend the day doing absolutely nothing without feeling guilty.

Appreciate singleness as God's gift to you right now. Wait on God for his direction. Meanwhile, honor God through your singleness. (On the other hand, being married doesn't let you off the hook. You still have a responsibility to serve God. It's just going to take more time and work because of the added responsibility of marriage.)

Moving On

We've taken you farther down your life path than you probably need to go right now, but that's OK. It doesn't hurt to think ahead. When it comes to your future, plan as if it depends on you, but pray and trust God as if it depends on him.

Now we're going to backtrack a bit to a more practical matter: *money.*

**It will seem like you are spending more and more
on less and less, until you are broke because
you spent everything on nothing.**

Tim P., age 22

CHAPTER 7

Money Matters—
Your Fiscal Fitness Program

Admit it. Until now, money hasn't been that much of a problem for you. Sure, there were times when you were running short. Maybe you couldn't go to the movie with your friends or you had to skimp on prom night (but the candle and floral arrangement on the table at McDonald's made it seem *just like* a fancy restaurant). Besides, if things got really tight, you could always play on your parents' sympathies. Maybe the conversation went something like this:

You: Mom, Dad, could I have a few bucks? Some friends and me want to go...

Them: That's "Some friends and *I*."

You: Yeah, whatever. Some friends and *I* want to go out to eat after the game.

Them: Why don't you spend your *own* cash for that? We aren't made of money, you know. It doesn't grow on trees. If all of your friends jumped off a cliff, would you ... Oh, wait, we got mixed up; we'll use that one for something else.

You : *(whining)* I never have enough money for anything.

Them: *(sarcastically)* We feel *sooo* sorry for you. You are *sooo* underprivileged.

Since your parents wouldn't give you any cash, maybe you "borrowed" the family's supermarket ATM card, bought a lot of cookies and pastries, and had your own little "bake sale for underprivileged kids" at school.

When you're on your own, the whole money thing changes. It gets worse. Money is harder to find and harder to keep. Everything costs more ... because *you're* paying for it. But don't worry. With a little planning, diligence, and self-deprivation on your part, and with a few practical and helpful tips on our part, you'll be able to afford everything that you need. Occasionally, just occasionally, you'll even be able to afford a few nonessential luxuries (like getting your dinner "super-sized" for an extra thirty-nine cents).

Factoid

What You've Cost So Far:

A government report estimates that middle-income families spend more than $150,000 to raise a child from birth to age seventeen.

The "Ups & Downs" and "Ins & Outs" of Money Management

Do you want to know:

- the simple secret for managing your money?
- the key to avoiding crippling debt and financial disaster?
- the miracle formula for affording everything that you own?

Of course you do. And we'll be glad to tell you. But the wisdom we're about to share with you is so plainly profound, yet so intensely insightful, that you must clear your mind of all other conflicting financial concepts. So, for the next few moments:

- Forget complicated economic theories (because they never seem to work when you're standing in the register line at the Gap).
- Ignore the bulls and bears of Wall Street (because we can never remember which one is good and which is bad).
- Avoid the "get rich quick" infomercials (with the testimonials by someone like Delores from Akron who bought a beachfront mansion for $1.97 at a government auction).

All you need to know and remember are four simple directions: in, out, up, and down. Here's how those four simple directions relate to managing your finances when you are living on your own:

> When your *outgo* exceeds your *income*,
> then your *upkeep* will be your *downfall*.

We can even make it simpler than that: Don't spend more than you make.

Would You Pay $1,259 for a Combo Meal?

If you spend more than you make, you'll be getting deeper in debt each day. Suppose that each day you spend just $3.45 (the cost of a #3 combo meal) more than you earn. That adds up to a little more than $100 a month. By the end of one year, you'll be in the hole $1,259. Now, that's a whopper of a debt for a hamburger.

"OPM" Can Be Dangerous to Your Health

Many people don't understand the concept that you have to live within your income. But think about it. If you aren't using *your* money, you have to be using someone *else's*. "Other people's money" (OPM) can be dangerous to your health because, sooner or later, the debts will all come due. You'll have nothing to pay them with, and you'll have to suffer the consequences.

Just in case you're tempted to reject our advice, let's take a look at what could happen if you try to take a ride on the OPM gravy train. Here is the list of your possible "donors" and "lenders." Look at the consequences that will follow if you take money from these sources without the ability to repay.

--- --- --- --- --- --- --- --- --- --- --- ---

Take God's Word for It
The wicked borrow and never repay.

--- --- --- --- --- --- --- --- --- --- --- ---

PSALM 37:21

Your Grandparents

Your "Nannie and Grandpappy" are probably the most sympathetic targets (oops, we mean prospects). Actually, you haven't called them "Nannie and Grandpappy" since you were four years old, but they always thought it was *so cute,* and now you'll do whatever it takes to kiss up to them.

But there are two big problems with hitting up your grandparents for money. First, they were your age two economic generations ago. Back then, you could buy a car for $25 (and they'll be glad to tell you about it, *again).* If you tell them you need $60 for a brand-name T-shirt, you may give them a coronary attack.

Second, you have to be prepared for a major guilt trip at every family reunion. You know, when your grandparents say something like: "We had to sell the family cemetery plots. Our finances are tight ever since we gave $60 to our favorite grandchild three years ago. It's a heartbreak for us, but we're glad to make the sacrifice. When we pass on, just dig a hole and bury us by the side of the road." Such comments seem a little disingenuous because your grandparents drove to the family reunion in a $400,000 motor home, but can you really live with that kind of guilt and pressure?

--- --- --- --- --- --- --- --- --- --- ---

Even if it is free, money from your relatives isn't worth the price you'll pay.

--- --- --- --- --- --- --- --- --- --- ---

FAQ: "What's wrong with being in debt? The government does it."

From your high-school civics or economics class, you remember the concept of deficit spending. This is what the federal government does. And after decades of spending more than its revenue, the U.S. government has a national debt of approximately a bazillion dollars (give or take a few trillion). But the federal government can operate in debt mode because it uses a few loopholes that aren't available to you.

- If the government needs more money, it prints it. If you print money, then debt won't be a problem for you because you can't buy anything in prison.

- If the government needs more money, it simply raises taxes. If you need more money, you can't raise the minimum wage.

- If the government needs more money, it takes it away from the Social Security reserves that your parents are counting on. If you need more money, you can't get it from your parents because they need all they've got in case Social Security goes bankrupt.

Your Friends

Your friends are probably as broke as you are. But let's assume that one of your friends was hit in the mouth at the age of seven by a neighbor kid's baseball. Thanks to a chipped tooth and a sleazy lawyer, your friend gets $10,000 of insurance money on his eighteenth birthday. He wants to spend it on college and cosmetic dental work, but you prevail upon your friendship to borrow $4,000 to pay your delinquent car payments and to cover your ebay.com auction bid of $1,829 for one of the backpacks from the movie *The Blair Witch Project*.

With only $6,000 left, your friend attends community college instead of

- - - - - - - - - - - - - - - -
**Borrowing money from a friend
may cost you the friendship!**
- - - - - - - - - - - - - - - -

his father's prestigious alma mater. Being greatly offended, the father revokes the offer to make your friend the vice president of his software company. Your friend has no direction in his life until he decides to become a fashion model. Fortunately, the Barbaricco's School of Modeling and Aloof Posture is holding auditions at a shopping mall in your town. Unfortunately, your friend's chipped smile is so repulsive that he becomes the first candidate that Barbaricco's has ever rejected.

Your Bank

You're dreaming if you think that you can get a loan from your bank. The bank will loan money to you only if you have enough assets ("collateral") or income ("high-paying job") to repay the loan. But if you had collateral or a high-paying job, you wouldn't need the loan. The bank doesn't make loans to people like you, which is why the bank has money and you don't.

But there are ways to get money from a bank without obtaining a loan. (No, we aren't suggesting anything that involves computer hacking or plastic explosives.) Maybe you have overdraft protection on your checking account or a credit card. By maxing out these sources, you could quickly find yourself in debt for several hundred dollars.

Unless you have the ability to repay, you will soon get a few nasty letters and then a few threatening phone calls. The bank is not interested in accepting those used CDs that you bought with its money, and you can't "work off" the debt by ironing twenty-dollar bills for the ATM. You might end up with a court judgment against you and a skull and crossbones icon on your credit report.

- - - - - - - - - - - - - - - - -

**Banks are in the business of *collecting* on loans.
Don't borrow money from your bank
unless you mean business.**

- - - - - - - - - - - - - - - - -

Vinnie Tuscalusso

He'll have a different name in your town, but we'll call him Vinnie Tusca-lusso. He is the unsavory guy who is always hanging around and can get you whatever you need ... for a price. In middle school, it might have been the answers to a history test. In high school, it was a forged off-campus pass. This guy is a walking Blockbuster store of bootleg videos and black-market CDs. (If you don't already know him, and we hope you don't, you can recognize him by the expensive-looking wristwatch he wears; it seems identical to a Rolex, but the watch face says "Rolax.")

Do not (we repeat: *do not*) do business with this guy. Oh, sure, he'll be glad to pay you $300 (in small denomination bills) for simply picking up a plain wrapped package from the lockers at the bus depot. But you'll regret it when you're arrested for carrying a box that contains the stolen computer chip for the high school's surveillance system. Or if you don't get caught at the bus station, you'll be apprehended a few weeks later by the FBI for pass-ing five-dollar bills with a picture of Adam Sandler wearing a beard and a stovepipe hat.

- - - - - - - - - - - - - - - - -
Don't borrow money from anyone who is anxious to loan it to you.
- - - - - - - - - - - - - - - - -

Your Parents

Your parents are a revenue source of last resort. In other words, don't even try. After all, they have been footing your bills through high school. After high school, they expect you to be all, or at least partially, on your own.

Give them a break. Shouldn't they be allowed to spend their limited dis-cretionary income on themselves? (You'll have to admit that your father is long overdue for new undershirts that will fit his ever-expanding abdomen. And your mother could replace those dresses that she has been wearing since you last listened to New Kids on the Block.)

If you don't heed our warnings and mistakenly ask your parents for money because you are spending more than you are making, then be prepared for the replay of several tracks from the *Parental Lectures—Greatest Hits* album:

- Track #4: When *I* was a kid, *my* parents couldn't afford to buy *me* anything.
- Track #7: Maybe you should get a second job.
- Track #16: You wouldn't need more money if you didn't spend it.
- Track #17: You don't need new clothes. Your sister's hand-me-downs will look fine on you, son.
- Track #22: Maybe you should get a second job. [Reprise]

Don't say we didn't warn you. If you refuse to take our advice, then you forfeit the right to roll your eyes back when the lecture begins. You asked for it, and listening to the "Parent Track" is the least you can do, since you both know that your parents won't ever be paid back.

Don't expect your parents to treat you like an adult if you keep asking them for money like a kid.

Put a Budget Belt Around Your Waste

Without a budget, you'll have a difficult time determining whether the cost of your lifestyle is exceeding your income. Until now, you probably didn't need a budget. Most of your expenses have been subsidized under the parental provision plan. Once you are on your own, however, your parents will pay for less and less. (Read that last sentence to mean: "Once you are on your own, however, *you* will be paying for more and more.")

A budget is a simple way of figuring out what you can afford. It helps you know how much of your revenue is committed to the essentials you have to pay for, and anything left over can be allocated for other things at your discretion. Budgeting is a simple process that goes as follows:

Schedule A: Your Income

Make a list of your monthly income. This may not take very long. If you have odd jobs that don't pay regularly, then do your best to estimate the monthly average. Be realistic. Sure, Aunt Isabel used to send you $20 on your birthday every year, but do you really expect that to continue after high school? (And, by the way, you must be really desperate if you are counting that $20 because it only counts for $1.66 of monthly income when spread out over the whole year.)

Schedule B: Your Expenses

We bet this list will be a lot longer. What do you have to pay for? Write the amount down for your monthly expenses. Some will always be the same (such as car payments), so that will be easy. Others vary each month, depending upon your mood, your appetite, and your car's mileage. So, for expenses such as food, clothes, and gasoline you may want to talk to someone who has been independent a while to help you make a reasonable estimate. You might have to adjust your estimates after a few months (after you have some "real life" experience with the bills).

Don't forget about expenses that don't get paid every month. For these bills (such as car insurance), you might only make two payments a year. Break these expenses down on a monthly basis. Maybe you pay college tuition at the beginning of each semester, but what is that amount per month? And don't just be thinking about you, you, you. What about planning for the charitable contributions that you will (or should) be making?

Avoid the Urge to Splurge

Living on a budget requires a great deal of self-discipline. You can only go for so long with the attitude that you are depriving yourself. (It is like being on a diet. After a while, you burst into Baskin-Robbins and order the 31 Flavors Sampler Platter.)

Don't think of your budget as a punishment. Otherwise, one day you'll buy a fifty-two-inch giant-screen TV because it was on special, even though it is too large to fit through the door in the double-wide mobile home you're renting.

Be honest with yourself. If all of the employees at Starbuck's know you as "double, tall, vanilla latte with skim milk, heated to 175 degrees," then estimate a lot more than just $15 a month as your "Food & Snacks" budget.

The Moment of Truth: Subtract Schedule B From Schedule A

If all goes well, the total on Schedule A will be more than the total on Schedule B. If it is, then:

1. Congratulations. You have extra spending money each month. Disburse the excess among the expense categories on Schedule B to give you a little extra "fudge" factor (figuratively or literally, depending upon your cravings). Or, put a new entry on Schedule B for something like "Getting Wild and Crazy" and then each month you can decide how to spend that extra $4.17. But before you actually spend any of that excess, read #2 below.

2. You are the first person in history who is unintentionally living within your means. You must have made a mistake. Go back and check your figures. Did you include *all* your expenses? (Your friends and family may not be too happy when they get no Christmas gifts from you. It will sound pretty lame for you to blame "budgetary design miscalculations.")

The Other Result

It is more likely that your expenses (Schedule B) exceed your income (Schedule A). Join the club. Now you've got to get financially creative in order to make the amounts equal each other. You have two choices:

1. *Make more income.* Wow, there is something you never thought of before. Don't spend too much time here. If there were something you could easily do to make more money, you'd probably already be doing it.

2. *Cut back on some of your expenses.* This is painful, but it is probably the only option for you. Maybe the first thing to go will be the $90 monthly expense for the daily "double, tall, vanilla latte with skim milk, heated to 175 degrees."

Using a Budget Is Different From *Having* a Budget

Lots of people *have* a budget. Few people *use* one. After you create your budget, then you have to live within its parameters. Sometimes that's fun, and sometimes it's not. If you have allocated $40 a month for clothes, and you only spend $30 in October, then you've got $50 to spend in November. On the other hand, if you have budgeted only a measly $25 a month for car repairs, a new radiator cap could throw your budget out of whack.

If you are over in one account, you'll have to stay under in another. So don't be so quick to spend that extra $10 of clothes money in October. You won't look good wearing a radiator cap, but it will work better than stuffing a sweater vest in the radiator hole.

Paper or Plastic?

The supermarket isn't the only place where this question applies. It is a key consideration once you are in charge of handling your own finances. Should you use paper (cash or checks) or plastic (charge cards)? Each system has its own advantages and drawbacks, but we think the checking account is the best choice if you are using a budget (notice we said *using* a budget).

Cash

You could cash your paycheck at the bank and walk around with a wad of bills. However, this presents obvious security problems if your wallet is lost or stolen. (And if you carry your wallet in your back pants pocket, the unsightly bulge will be a fashion *faux pas.*)

If you are spending cash, it is hard to keep track of where it goes. To stay on a budget, at the beginning of the month you could put the cash into separate envelopes for each expense item. For example, if you're planning on spending $50 each month for gas, you put $50 in the envelope marked "Gas" and keep it in the glove compartment of your car. When you use up the money in the envelope, you stop buying gas for the month. (Just hope you aren't two hundred miles from home on the interstate when your gas tank and your gas envelope simultaneously go empty.)

Credit Cards

Credit cards have the convenience of giving you buying power without carrying a wad of cash in your pocket. (No unsightly bulges.) They also have the advantage of giving you a written record (the receipt and your monthly statement) for where your money went. This makes budgeting much easier and more accurate.

The disadvantage of credit cards is their illusion that you have more money than your budget may allow. When store clerks accept your credit card, they will never ask, "Are you sure this expenditure is within the parameters of your budgetary constraints?" You've got to keep track of your expenditures during the month so you won't be surprised (and your budget won't be obliterated) when the bill comes the next month.

Unsolicited Solicitations

Credit card companies *love* college students. Not *love* as in a "have affection for" kind of way, but *love* as in "make a lot of money off of" kind of way. Most college students, not having read this book, don't have the discipline to control their spending. The credit card companies can be pretty sure that the college student will run the card balance to the credit limit and then get stuck paying double-digit interest (and late-payment penalty fees) for years to come.

So, be prepared for mass mailings of credit card offers. You'll get them all: the general ones (such as Visa, MasterCard, and Discover Card) and the specialty variety (gasoline companies, department stores, and your local Video Schmideo Store).

We suggest that you pick one with a low limit, for emergencies only, and pay it off each month without fail. Now, here's the really important part: *Throw all of the other solicitations away.* After you start your own Internet company, then you can have two: one for personal use and another for business. But for now, one is enough.

Checking Account

Once you are on your own, a checking account is a necessity. It is the safest way to hold your money (in the bank instead of your wallet), and it gives you an immediate record of what you spend your money for (assuming that you make a notation in the ledger every time you write a check). Of course, the total in your checkbook ledger won't be reliable unless you follow a few rules:

- *Write it down right away.* Take the extra seventeen seconds to write the check number, payee, description, and amount in the ledger when you write the check. Who cares if some impatient doofus is standing behind you in the grocery store checkout line? You won't remember that information later that evening after you eat dinner and fall asleep watching the syndicated rerun of "Friends."

- *Reconcile your statement each month.* This just means checking your ledger total against the total on your monthly bank statement. DO NOT JUST CHANGE THE TOTAL IN YOUR CHECKBOOK LEDGER TO MATCH THE BANK STATEMENT LEDGER. You have to subtract from the bank statement total any "outstanding" checks that haven't gone through the bank yet. So, if your bank statement total says $487.29, remember that the bank doesn't yet know about that $59.83 check you wrote to the Home Shopping Network for that three-bottle set of "Forever Tanfastic Tanning Solution—Formula II."

- *Watch those debit cards.* These cards are like charge cards, except when the clerk swipes the card the money is swiped immediately from your checking account. There is nothing wrong with them, but you need to remember to write the amount of the charge in your checkbook ledger. These cards are a relatively painless way to spend money. That's the problem with them.

Separation Anxiety: An Out-of-Town Bank
Suppose you open a checking account at your hometown bank. Great! No problem ... until you go away to college. Sometimes merchants won't accept a check written on an out-of-town bank. It may be a hassle even to buy groceries. The solution: use an interstate bank or open a bank account in the city where you attend college.

ATM Anonymity

Even if you use a checking account and a credit card, you'll need cash from time to time ... usually when the banks are closed. Get an ATM card so you can have access to cash on a twenty-four-hour basis. (When a midnight craving hits, you've got to feed it!) We know you'll have a lot on your mind with college classes and maybe a job, but save a little cranial capacity for your PIN number. Here are two PIN precautions:

- *If you get to choose your own PIN number, use a little creativity.* Don't use your birth date (because your ATM will probably be stolen with your driver's license, and birthdays are the most obvious choice).

- *If you need to write it down, don't make your PIN too easy for someone else to find.* If you have to write your PIN number down to remember it, don't keep the slip of paper in your wallet, and don't write the number on the ATM card (even if you use that backwards-mirror writing).

Finally, for safety's sake, try to avoid late-night trips to the cash machine. Or if you have to get cash late at night, don't go to the machine alone. The "buddy system" works as well in this situation as when you're swimming in the ocean, and for much the same reason: when you're looking for sharks, two sets of eyes are always better than one.

Affording College: It Takes Money to Make Money

Your biggest expense over the next few years is going to be college. As we discussed in Chapter Two, there are lots of reasons to go to college. But from strictly a financial standpoint, a college education is a wise investment because most college graduates make much more money during their working lives than those without college degrees.

Cost: Last but Not Least

When you are choosing which college or university to attend, the cost is not the *least* important factor, but it should be the *last* factor you consider. We mean that your decision should first be made without considering the cost.

Decide which particular college or university is best for you based on the many nonfinancial factors mentioned in Chapter Two. (Do you want a small college or a large university? Which school has the best program for the major you are interested in? Christian or secular? Private or public? Liberal arts or research and technology?)

After you have decided on the institution that will best equip you for the kind of person you want to be and the career you're interested in, *then* look at the cost.

If your parents get a hold of this book, they'll probably rip out this section. They'll say that college expenses are a major part of the decision process. We agree, but we think that there is not one big decision. There are two separate decisions:

Decision #1:

Which is the best college or institution for you
(ignoring financial considerations)?

After you have the answer to Decision #1, then you move to the second stage:

Decision #2:

How can you make the financial arrangements
for the school you have selected?

Paying Less Than the Cost

Very few college students pay the full amount of what their college education costs. It is not uncommon for 80 to 90 percent of the student population to be on some form of assistance. Here are a few of the financial aid opportunities that may be available to you at the institution of your choice:

- *Academic scholarships:* Many schools will provide a scholarship toward tuition if your GPA and SAT or ACT scores are high enough. The brainiacs can get a full ride, but even the less-than-genius types can receive a major discount. These scholarships may be unrelated to financial need.

- *Athletic scholarships:* Sports programs play a major role in college life. Each school's reputation and publicity is tied in to the success of its sports teams. If you are really good at running or jumping or throwing, the school may pay to get you on their team.

- *Other scholarships:* If you're in the middle of the pack academically and athletically, don't despair. There are a lot of scholarships awarded based on other criteria. Maybe your college has a scholarship for mediocre students with blond hair who major in kinesiology. You have the mediocre part covered, and a stop at the drug store can take care of the blond hair color, and you're sure you'll want to major in kinesiology (as soon as someone explains what it is).

- *Grants:* Federal and state grants (money that you don't have to pay back) are available on the basis of financial need.

- *Loans:* Loans from the federal and state governments and from the school may be available. These loans have to be paid back, but they are usually at low interest or no interest. The repayment schedule usually begins after graduation (which is a built-in incentive for you to go to work after college).

- *Work-study:* Where do you think the college gets its cheap labor force? Someone has to spread the fertilizer on the grass and dish out the green beans in the dining commons (usually these are separate jobs).

Here's the point of all of this: There are lots of ways to accomplish the financing of your college education. Contact the Financial Aid Office and investigate all of the options. It will be the best investment you ever make.

Moving On

All the money in the world won't do you much good if you are nailed shut in a pine box buried six feet under and pushing up daisies. We know that "health" isn't something you think about very often. Until this point in your life, you haven't had to. Your mother took care of that (with the vitamin C at breakfast and broccoli at dinner). But once you are on your own, you are responsible for your own health. That could be a scary thought, so the next chapter will help you figure out how to stay alive (and we won't mention broccoli once).

CHAPTER 8

Healthy Choices—
Preparing Your Body to Last a Lifetime

We've gotten to know each other pretty well by now, haven't we? You've stuck with us for more than half the book, which means you are becoming very familiar with our philosophy of life. Actually, we haven't given you our *exact* philosophy of life yet, so now might be a good time.

Bruce & Stan's Philosophy of Life

L: *Live for God.* He's given you his best, so give him your best.

I: *Invest in people.* In the end it's the only investment that pays eternal dividends.

F: *Focus on a goal.* You'll never get anywhere if you don't know where you're going.

E: *Every day counts.* Today really is the first day of the rest of your life.

Just as you've gotten to know us and what we're about, we like to think that we know you and a little of what you're about. For example, we know that you have all sorts of dreams and goals for your life. We suspect you want to make your mark in this world. And we hope you desire to serve God wholeheartedly.

That's a tall order for anyone. Accomplishing all you want to accomplish and doing everything you want to do is going to take commitment, hard work, perseverance, and time. Oh, and it's going to take one more thing: *a healthy body*.

You're Not Going to Live Forever

Well, at least your *body* isn't. Your *soul*—the spiritual part of you—is going to live forever (more about that in Chapter Eleven). But your body is an entirely different matter.

Everything about your body is finite. There are limitations. If you take care of your body, it should serve you well for seventy, eighty, even ninety years. (If you make one hundred, Willard Scott will slap your name and photo on the side of a Smuckers jar.)

There are no guarantees, of course, that you won't contract a life-threatening disease or get hit by a train. Sometimes things happen, and we don't know the reason (for example, no one has yet figured out what being a centenarian has to do with jam). But there is plenty you can do to care for the amazing physical body God has given you.

Start Thinking Healthy

Up until now you've been blessed with a young and strong body. You've been able to eat junk food, dive into mosh pits, and basically sit around without any serious damage to your system. When you participate in a strenuous outdoor activity, such as hiking, water-skiing, or bowling, you wake up the next morning without feeling stiff (believe us, that won't always be the case).

It's a remarkable machine, your body. About the only down side your body has experienced is the presence of acne, and that's fading quickly. So you better enjoy it while you still can. And while you're at it, why not start planning for the rest of your life right now?

Choose to steer clear of risky behavior and destructive habits. That doesn't mean you have to settle for a boring, low-key life. We're not asking you to play it *safe*. We're asking you to play it *smart*. All the dreams and desires in the world won't mean a thing if you abuse your body. What good is standing on top of the world if you're on your last leg? "Don't you realize that all of you together are the temple of God and that the Spirit of God lives in you?" (1 Cor 3:16).

Take care of yourself. From the standpoint of wear and tear, these are the best days your body will ever have. There will never be a better time to begin the habits of healthy living.

It's like starting a savings account. If you put twenty bucks a week into savings now, you'll have a comfortable retirement. If you wait until you retire to start saving, it won't help you a bit. Same goes for your body. If you begin now to establish a lifetime of health, you'll enjoy the dividends of health for a lifetime.

Why Bring It Up Now?

Why deal with health issues now? Can't it wait until after you're through school and in the routine of a job and eventually a family? No, this can't wait. Here are two reasons:

1. The *bad* habits you start now will *hinder* you for the rest of your life.

2. The *good* habits you start now will *help* you for the rest of your life.

You more or less fall into bad habits without realizing it. They sneak up on you in small ways and become a part of your routine over time. Some bad habits are annoying but harmless:

- Uncle Charlie's habit of sucking through his teeth in a futile attempt to dislodge particles of food that have been there since last Christmas,

- Cousin Billy's habit of hocking up lugis and then swallowing them, and
- your habit of never making your bed (unlike the habits of Uncle Charlie and Cousin Billy, this only annoys one person—your mom).

Other habits are harmless most of the time but have the potential to get a person into trouble:
- Grandpa's habit of backing up in traffic without looking,
- your neighbor's habit of letting his dog poop on your lawn, and
- your habit of always being ten minutes late.

Then there are those habits that seem harmless enough at first and don't seem to have any immediate consequences. However, over time, there is an absolute certainty that any one of these habits will lead to serious consequences and negative health issues.

Eating

Research has proven that if you ingest too much fat, too many calories, and too much cholesterol into your system, you will do damage to your body in the long haul. One of the advantages you have is a resilient body. You may eat so many burgers and fries at Wendy's that Dave Thomas sends you a Christmas card each year. And yet you've been able to maintain your weight and healthy glow.

Here are some of the ways your eating habits will get you in the end (sorry) unless you develop better ones *now*.

Eating the wrong things. There's an old saying: *You are what you eat.* If that were true, many Americans would look like a pizza or a French fry (come to think of it, many of them do). Actually, the truth in that statement is that your health—and to a large extent your appearance—is directly related to the foods you eat.

Twenty years ago the health food craze had not yet kicked in. Except for Euell Gibbons and his wild hickory nuts (you're not old enough to remember Euell, but your parents are), or maybe that crusty old guy with the furry mustache extolling the virtues of Quaker Oats, nobody thought too much about eating healthy foods. Today things have changed. We know better. Research has proven that you will be a healthier person if you eat healthy foods.

Bad Habits Start Early

Want to know why there are so many fat little kids around (how's that for an oxymoron)? Biomedical researcher Catherine Champagne thinks she knows why. More than one-fourth of the vegetables eaten by children are potato chips and French fries. For teenagers the amount of fried potatoes consumed as a percentage of total vegetables eaten goes up to 33 percent.

Hear us now, believe us later. If you continue to eat with abandon through your prime years, we guarantee that your waistline (if you're a guy) or hips (if you're a girl) will have a larger circumference than they do now. And that's just on the *outside*. Only God (and eventually your doctor) knows what's going on in the *inside*.

Eating too much. The biggest eating problem most Americans have—and this includes most people your age—is that they eat too much. Unless you're an athlete in serious training or you are blessed with the metabolism of a hummingbird, you probably don't need to eat as much as you do. Here are some guidelines for those who overachieve in the eating arena:

- Don't eat until you're stuffed; eat until you're full.
- Don't go back for seconds. Or thirds.
- Skip dessert unless it's your birthday.
- Don't eat snacks before you go to bed.
- Keep healthy snacks in your room to munch on when you're hungry during the day.

The Sin of Gluttony

Gluttony—literally *excess eating*—is listed in classic literature as one of the "Seven Deadly Sins." The Bible pretty much puts it in the same category as drunkenness: "Do not carouse with drunkards and gluttons, for they are on their way to poverty" (Prv 23:20-21).

Not eating enough. Skipping meals because you're too busy or starving yourself because you suddenly think you're overweight is really dumb. And destructive. Eating disorders among kids have been well publicized, and they are serious matters that require professional help. But you don't have to be suffering from anorexia or bulimia to do damage to your body. Going on crash diets is never a good idea; besides, you always gain back the weight.

In addition to bad eating habits, there are a few other bad habits (in some cases, both unhealthy and illegal) that will take their toll on your health. Guaranteed.

Smoking
Smoking is such a stupid and destructive habit that we shouldn't have to talk about it. But the ridiculous fact is that kids your age are smoking in ever-increasing numbers.

Factoid
Studies show that half of the smokers who began smoking when they were teenagers will reduce their life expectancies by twenty to twenty-five years.

If you know why young adults smoke, please tell us (our E-mail address is in the back of the book). Frankly, we're at a loss as to why anyone—especially someone in the prime of life—would smoke. Maybe it's the special physical qualities, that mysterious allure, that smoking gives you:

- yellow teeth and fingers
- bad breath
- pale, crinkly skin
- a delightful cough
- reduced lung capacity
- reduced life expectancy

Or maybe it's just the idea that smoking puts you in control. With very little effort, you effectively put your life and the lives of those around you in mortal danger. What power!

Around 30 percent of all eighteen- to twenty-five-year-olds smoke. If you're one of them, well, we think you know how we feel (hey, we still love you, but we want you around for a while). If one or more of your friends smoke, don't be mean about it, but express your concerns. If they refuse to quit, our advice would be to get up and leave every time they light up.

Smoke at Home

What do you do if someone in your family smokes, especially one or both of your parents? Treat them with love and respect, but definitely voice your concerns for their health (not to mention yours). Tell them that no matter how long they've smoked, it's never too late to quit. The health benefits of quitting abound, regardless of age.

Drinking

Drinking is a pretty controversial subject. "Social" drinking is acceptable in most circles, including some religious ones (frankly, the Bible doesn't prohibit drinking, it just instructs us not to get drunk). On the other hand, some people believe that it's never right to drink because of where it can lead you.

We want to strike a little balance by suggesting two things:

1. If you're under age, never drink. Don't even try.
2. Just because you're able to drink, don't think you have to. Don't buckle under peer pressure (there's plenty of it, no matter how old you are).

Even though you think you can "handle" it, you need to be aware that everyone who ends up with a drinking problem once thought he or she could handle it. And it doesn't take a long time to go from nothing to having a real problem.

The fact of the matter is that drinking is a real problem among college-age people. Here's some sobering information from *College Clues for the Clueless:*[1]

- Student drinking is the number-one health problem on college campuses today.
- Alcohol is a "factor" in 41 percent of all academic problems.
- Ninety percent of rapes occur while either the rapist or the victim is "under the influence" of alcohol.
- If there's a crime on campus, alcohol is usually involved.

Even though you might not have a drinking problem, you probably know someone who does. According to a landmark Harvard University study on the effects of drinking on college students, 67 percent of all students have experienced at least one "adverse consequence" as a result of another student's drinking.

Drugs

Unfortunately, drugs and college students seem to go together. Ever since Professor Timothy Leary (ask your parents about him, right after you ask them about Euell Gibbons) suggested that America's youth "tune in, turn on, drop out" through mind-altering drugs, an alarming number of students have done just that.

Why do students turn to drugs? Psychologists suggest that any one of the following anxieties can contribute to drug use: personal pressure, insecurity, loneliness, and the need to "belong."

- - - - - - - - - - - - - - -
Coincidence?
Thirty percent of all eighteen- to twenty-five-year-olds
in the United States smoke. Just over 30 percent of
all college students used marijuana last year.
- - - - - - - - - - - - - - -

Even if you don't use drugs, you will probably run into someone who does. According to *College Clues for the Clueless,* here are some signs to look for:

- poor personal health
- noticeable weight loss
- inconsistent class attendance
- radical mood swings
- anxiety and nervousness
- no longer dependable
- always financially strapped

Risky Business

Destructive habits develop out of risky behavior. It's only natural that you should want to take risks in your life, whether it's in class selection, sports, business, or travel.

That's not what we're talking about. Risky behavior that leads to bad habits comes from the proverbial "being at the wrong place at the wrong time." Places where sex, drinking, and drugs are not only available but encouraged. You don't have to go to some dark place of ill repute to find opportunities to engage in such behavior.

The place where you will likely be tempted to do the wrong thing is the classic party. Not all parties are bad, but many are basically trouble waiting to happen . . . to you. Even if you don't get caught doing something you shouldn't on any given night, risky behavior always leads to destructive habits.

Good Habits, Good Results

Before we get to our list of the Top Three constructive health habits, we want to make sure you understand something. Let's put it in the form of a Bruce & Stan Truism:

Your good habits will be much more effective if you eliminate your bad habits.

We're not saying that you need to get rid of every bad habit before you can start good habits (if that were the case, we'd all be in trouble). What we are saying is that where your body is concerned, the good stuff you put in will be much more effective if you stop putting bad stuff in.

Let's go through the Good Habits. These aren't so difficult. In fact, they're easy. And that's what we call them, EEZEE:

E:	Eating right
E:	Exercising regularly
ZEE:	Sleeping enough

Eating Right

Earlier in this chapter we encouraged you to play it *smart*. This is especially true when it comes to eating for healthy results. We aren't experts in this field, but there are plenty of people who are. We recommend Cheryl Townsley's book, *Food Smart.*[2] Here are ten tips for healthy eating:

1. Eat more vegetables.
2. Eat more fruits.
3. Eat food in the healthiest form possible.
4. Drink fresh juices when possible.
5. Reduce your intake of sugar.
6. Reduce fats.
7. Eat whole-grain pastas and breads.
8. Reduce your intake of meat.
9. Eat less dairy.
10. Drink more water.

Cheryl also recommends that you avoid these foods: caffeine, alcohol, foods with preservatives or additives, high-sodium products, MSG, refined sugar, white flour, margarine, white rice, carbonated beverages, and smoked foods.

How to Avoid the Freshman Fifteen

The famous "Freshman Fifteen" describes what happens when students leave home for college and start eating like Homer Simpson. Before you know it, they begin to *look* like Homer Simpson.

It's easy to avoid gaining those fifteen extra pounds. Most college cafeterias have improved their selections tremendously, adding healthy foods and juices to the menu. All you have to do is eat smart, avoiding such waistline expanders as junk food snacks and late-night burger binges. Stock your own healthy snacks for those times when you do get the munchies.

Exercise

In her excellent book, *Greater Health God's Way*, Stormie Omartian says that "exercise is just as important in weight loss as proper diet."[3] Eating healthy will help you, but when you combine your good eating habits with a regular exercise routine, you'll maintain or even lose your weight while keeping your rosy glow.

When we say "exercise," we don't mean fanatical, endorphin-popping, budget-breaking exercise that takes hours of time and hundreds of dollars. We're talking about

- walking, jogging, or running;
- bicycling;
- sensible weight training; and
- team sports (such as basketball, volleyball, and tennis).

The important thing is to choose something you enjoy and then follow Nike's advice: *Just do it!*

Sleep

Sleep is very underrated as a factor in health. The truth is that your body—including your brain—repairs and rebuilds itself during sleep. And the truth is also that, when you get on your own, it's like you never want to sleep! There are so many new experiences, so many things to do, so many new people to meet. And then when you think you've done everything you possibly can in a twenty-four-hour period, you realize you have to study. So you pull an "all-nighter." And after several weeks of this crazy routine, you wonder why you're feeling lousy or even downright sick.

Bruce Talks About His Students

I'm a practicing attorney, but I also teach a class on leadership at Westmont College in Santa Barbara, California. At the beginning of each semester I see the same pattern: the students are fresh, alert, eager, and well rested. Then, after about six weeks, the inevitable happens. Baggy eyes, runny noses, and nodding heads (and I'm not talking nods of approval or understanding) characterize the class, causing many to miss class altogether (and it's such a shame to miss even one minute of my instruction). I would say that the culprit in this change of health and well-being is lack of sleep. That and a failure on the part of the young men to do laundry on a regular basis.

Now we're not going to suggest that you get eight hours of sleep every night. That's too much to ask. But you can do better than the four or five hours you're getting now. Here are our Top Ten ways to help you stay healthy by getting enough sleep (with a little help from Stormie Omartian):

1. Eat healthy foods.

2. Get enough exercise.

3. Take little breaks during the day.

4. Avoid caffeine (including sodas).

5. Avoid alcohol.

6. Get plenty of fresh air.

7. Take a short nap during the day (but not in class).

8. Make sure you have enough ventilation.

9. If your dorm or apartment is noisy, get earplugs.

10. Go to bed earlier than everyone else.

Despite your best efforts to establish good habits (make no mistake about it, effort is required), you're going to "backslide." You're going to slip back into those crummy habits of eating poorly, going without enough sleep, and possibly even putting harmful stuff in your body. Why? Oh, there are lots of reasons, but we've got a simple one. We've seen it in our own lives, and we think we see it in yours. It's called overcommitment.

You want to do well and you want to do it all. You make too many promises, and you try to please too many people. So you eat on the run, pull an all-nighter, drink a lot of caffeine, take No-Doze—and before you know it, you're a physical, emotional, and spiritual wreck. And if you're in school, your grades aren't too hot either.

Too many commitments cause stress, and stress causes your body to do strange things. Your heart races, your blood pressure rises, your muscles tighten, your appetite increases or decreases, and often your mood changes. Not good. You need a way to manage stress.

Managing Stress: It's All in Your Mind

Just like everything else in this chapter, managing stress is a matter of bringing balance to your life and using your head. You don't need to make an appointment with a medical doctor or a psychologist (unless you're demonstrating some serious symptoms) in order to reduce your stress. Just use some common sense. Hey, if you'd have thought about it long enough, you could have come up with these seven stress busters:

- Eat healthy foods.
- Exercise regularly.
- Get enough sleep.
- Get organized.
- Learn to say "no."
- Talk it out.
- Pray.

While you won't be able to eliminate your stress—no one ever has—you can successfully manage it. And the result will be a healthier, happier life.

Nurture It
OK, we've given you plenty of advice on feeding your *body* and keeping it healthy. If you follow the tips we've compiled, your *emotions* will improve as well. Now it's time to put a ribbon around this chapter by talking about your *mind*. We can almost guarantee you that if you keep your mind healthy, your body and emotions will follow.

- - - - - - - - - - - - - - -
What goes into the mind comes out in the life.
- - - - - - - - - - - - - - -

Bill Anderson

Time to Renew
Did you know that the Bible makes a direct connection between your body and your mind? Long before scientists and psychologists came up with the notion that your mind is a powerful force in your well being, the apostle Paul wrote:

And so, dear brothers and sisters, I plead with you to give your bodies to God. Let them be a living and holy sacrifice—the kind he will accept. When you think of what he has done for you, is this too much to ask? Don't copy the behavior and customs of this world, but let God transform you into a new person by changing the way you think. Then you will know what God wants you to do, and you will know how good and pleasing and perfect his will really is.

ROMANS 12:1-2

The Art of Spiritual Breathing

The way you present your body to God is to allow him to transform you by changing the way you think. How does that happen? You practice the art of *spiritual breathing.*

Inhale the Word of God

If God is going to change you, he has to speak to you. And the way he speaks to you is through his personal message to you—his Word, the Bible. If you're longing to hear from God, you can, as often and as much as you want. All it takes is reading the Bible.

All Scripture is inspired by God and is useful to teach us what is true and to make us realize what is wrong in our lives. It straightens us out and teaches us to do what is right. It is God's way of preparing us in every way, full equipped for every good thing God wants us to do.

2 TIMOTHY 3:16-17

When you bring God's Word into your life through your mind, you give the Holy Spirit an opportunity to work in your life, to change the way you think so you can glorify God.

Exhale Prayer

If God talks to you through his Word, the way you talk to God is through prayer. Someone once said that prayer moves the hand that moves the world.

Prayer is an awesome thing because it literally puts you into the presence of the living God. Prayer isn't speaking in formal language or reading from a script. Prayer is talking to God from your heart, thanking him, voicing your concerns, and asking help for others.

Like reading your Bible, the results of prayer are greater if you are consistent. That doesn't mean God won't respond to your sporadic and desperate pleas, but he loves to hear from you every day, several times a day, no matter where you are or what you are doing. Prayer is the foundation of a vibrant relationship with the living God. It is also a key to renewing your mind.

Imagine for a moment what you would look like and how you would feel if you made the decision to give your body, your mind, and your spirit the best you possibly can every single day. Even more, think about the influence you would have on the world around you. Your potential would be virtually limitless.

Moving On

In this and the preceding chapters, we have been talking about the "new you": new address, new friends, new experiences, new adventures.

But there is a part of the "old you" that still lingers behind and shouldn't be forgotten. We're talking about your family. You remember them—those parents and siblings whom you have been living with for eighteen years. Even though you will be off to bigger and better things, they will still play a big part in your life after high school. The dynamics of those relationships, however, will never be the same.

In Chapter Nine, we'll give you a little insight about how those relationships will change so you can be prepared for it before it happens.

CHAPTER 9

Family Ties—
Out of Sight, but Not Forgotten

When you reach that senior year in high school, you are feeling pretty secure. You've got the high-school studying thing down pat (which doesn't necessarily mean that you are studying; it may mean that you know how to get by without studying). You've mastered the art of making friends (and knowing what kind of people you should avoid) on campus.

By the spring semester of your senior year, you are even learning how to communicate with your parents and understand them. Well, "understanding" may be a bit of a stretch; let's just accept the fact that you are communicating with them much better than in your previous teenage years. Your life has a nice, tranquil feeling to it.

Then, in less time than it takes to unzip your rented graduation robe, there are going to be some drastic changes. Not everything changes. Some things stay the same. If you're going to college, you'll still have to contend with studying (and your college classes may be very similar to your old high-school classes; even those desk-and-chair combos are the same size). And making friends and avoiding enemies isn't going to be all that much different either.

The dramatic changes in your life are going to happen in your home. Oh, your mom and dad will still be your parents, and your brothers and sisters will still be your siblings, but the dynamics of your relationship will change, and it will never, ever go back to the way it was before.

Singing the Parental Postpartum Blues

After childbirth, many women suffer from "postpartum depression." Even though they have a cherub-looking infant, who is wrapped in swaddling clothes and cradled safely in their arms, they are distraught and despondent over the little critter's departure from the womb. As you get ready to leave home and move out on your own, the emotional scenario could be worse—because now your dad may be blubbering, too.

Whether you are moving out to go to college or to begin "life on your own," those last few months will be traumatic for your parents. Like flash-back scenes in a movie, their minds will be filled with tender memories of you:

- the time you stuck a marble up your nose and had to be taken to the emergency room;

- your first ride on a two-wheeler bike without training wheels, when your dad was so exhausted from running alongside you that *he* had to be taken to the emergency room;

- your first day of kindergarten, when your mom picked out your clothes and dressed you;

- your last day of high school, when your mom wished she had picked out your clothes and dressed you;

- the day you passed your driver's license test ... on the second try (mental pictures from the first test day have been deleted from their memories); and

- the day you scored the winning goal and your soccer team won the championship (actually, you didn't score the winning goal, but that's not the way your parents are going to remember it).

With all of these memories pulsating through their hearts and minds, they are going to be emotional wrecks even before the door closes behind you. Be prepared for emotional mood swings and erratic behavior.

How to Say Good-bye

Picture the scene in your mind: Your parents have unloaded the car at college, and all of your gear is moved into the dorm room (or maybe the U-Haul is parked on the street outside your new apartment). You are standing there with your roommate, excited about beginning a new adventure.

Then you look over and see your parents with a morose look on their faces. Your mom is frantically looking for a tissue in her purse, and your dad is pretending that the tears in his eyes are from the smog in the air. Simply put, they are emotional wrecks. They are acting as if they have lost their best friend. In a way, that is exactly what has happened.

When you first move out of the house, it may not seem so emotional to you. After all, you may only be a short drive away. But this event marks an emotional moment for your parents, so take a few moments to spend with them. Don't get so wrapped up in the adventure of your new life that you overlook how your parents are feeling.

Look at It From Your Parents' Perspective
Your parents have survived your progression from diapers to diploma. During that time it was *you* who made most of the changes. Now, all of a sudden, it is your parents who will have to make the most dramatic adjustments. Sure, you will continue to change a little bit at a time as you make the transition into adulthood, but your parents will have to go through a major role change. They have spent almost two decades as "hands-on" managers. After your graduation from high school, their position will change drastically to that of an "outside consultant."

Here's how you see it. When you begin life out on your own, whether as a college student or as a working adult, you will be leading a relatively independent life.

- You will expect that "rules" are replaced by your own emphasis on personal responsibility.
- You will view freedom as a necessary component of your maturing process.
- You will consider that your personal independence overshadows any vestiges of obligation or accountability to your parents.
- You will resent continued intrusion and meddling in your life by your parents.

These are all natural, reasonable, and understandable feelings on your part. But they are completely opposite from your parents' perspective.

This is your parents' viewpoint. You might think of yourself as an adult, but your parents have all those memories of you being a goofy, irresponsible kid. When you start to assert your independence and take offense when they impose restrictions, you're likely to hear comments such as:

- "You are still just a kid."
- "Is this the thanks we get for all our slaving and sacrifice?"

And the infamous:

- "As long as you are living in our house, you'll play by our rules."

These are all natural, reasonable, and understandable feelings for your parents to have. (Remember, they heard the same things from *their parents*. It is kind of a thirty-year déjà vu thing.)

Be Patient With Your Parents; They Are Slow Learners

Particularly if you are the oldest child, your parents are going to be struggling to learn their new role in life. They are no longer wardens or even coaches. When you are out and on your own, they are sort of like a concierge—they are standing by, anxious to help and advise you, but only if you come to them with questions.

You can help your parents through this difficult transition if you are sensitive to the transformation they must make:

- *They're learning to "check in" with you instead of "checking up" on you.* They will be curious about what is going on in your life. (You'll agree that there is nothing wrong with that.) They know that you are responsible for your own actions, and they know you will be resentful if they are perceived as monitoring. So give them the benefit of the doubt. Assume that their inquiries are made from their heartfelt curiosity and are not intended to be judgmental.

- *They're learning to listen instead of lecture.* For eighteen years, they were doing the talking, and you were (supposed to be) doing the listening. But after you graduate from high school, they must flip-flop and suddenly be quick to listen and slow to speak. They are anxious to develop an adult-to-adult relationship with you that fosters communication. They know that this won't happen if every conversation with you ends with a parental discourse on sleep, studies, and socializing. But give them a break. Realize that old habits die hard.

- *They're learning to give advice only when asked.* Your parents are painfully aware that you still have much to learn. You won't deny this fact, but you'd like to learn some of it on your own. There's the problem. Your parents have an extra generation of experience from which they know you can benefit. They don't want you making the same mistakes that they made, so they are anxious to bless you with their sage wisdom and knowledge. But be patient. Sooner or later they will learn that you will be much more receptive to their advice when you decide to ask for it. (Periodically, just for the fun of it, ask your parents a "What do you think I should do?" question. They will feel *so* fulfilled.)

- *They're learning to ask questions for the sake of praying, not for prying.* All of a sudden, your parents have to abandon the litany of "who, what, when" cross-examination techniques which they developed when you were in high school. They know that they are more likely to get information out of you now if they phrase their questions in a more generic form, such as, "How would you like me to be praying for you?"

- *They're learning to let you live under their roof but not under their thumb.* If you are living away from home, the hardest adjustment will be on those weekends, holidays, and vacations when you return home. Your parents will have memories and recollections of the rules that were in place during high school, but you will have been living in a relatively unrestricted environment. Maybe your parents won't feel a need to impose the old "rules of the house" if you are quick to display courtesy and respect by letting them know what you will be doing and where you will be going.

Your parents' love for you won't diminish when you become an adult and leave home, but the way in which they interact with you will be drastically different. There is a delicate art to this transition: mothering without monitoring, loving without leading, and interacting without intruding. Your parents understand the distinctions, but it may take them a while to make the transformation. Give them a little slack.

Keeping Your Parents in the Loop

Despite all of the jokes about gaining an extra bedroom, your parents are going to be sad when you leave home. After all, they stuck by you when you were going through those rebellious, snotty teenage years. Now, just when you're becoming an adult and your parents are enjoying your friendship at that level, you're moving out. How rude!

It will be hard on your parents because they will feel as if they are losing a friend. They will feel "out of the loop" because they don't know what is going on in your life. But you can solve that problem with these simple four steps:

Step 1: *Buy a disposable camera.* Take pictures of your new friends and your activities and send some photos to your parents. Hey, your parents may even pay for the camera and the developing as an incentive to get the pictures. (Remember double prints: One for you and one for them.)

Step 2: *Send them a copy of your college newspaper.* You won't read everything in the paper, but your parents will. They will be able to live your college life vicariously through each issue.

Step 3: *Send them a copy of your class schedule.* You don't have a difficult time getting a mental picture of where your parents are because you are totally familiar with their jobs and their schedules. But if you are away at college, they won't know anything about your daily schedule unless you tell them. If you send them a copy of your class schedule, we bet that you will see it stuck to the refrigerator door when you return home.

Step 4: *Invite them to come and visit you.* They could go overboard with this, so you will have to use caution. If you leave for your freshman year of college on September *1st*, they'll be ready to come for a visit by about September *6th*. We think that is a little too soon (and we know that you will think it is *way* too soon). But by the end of October or the first part of November, you will have made lots of new friends whom your parents have never met. They'll be eager to visit you, and they certainly won't deny your request that they take you and your friends out for dinner at a nice restaurant. (Even if you aren't anxious to see your parents, you'll be glad for a meal away from the campus dining commons.)

If you are living in an apartment or dorm in your hometown, the same rule applies. They will be glad to spend time with you and your friends because they are interested in getting an "update" on what's happening in your life.

You've Got E-mail

It is our humble (and correct) opinion that E-mail is the best way to stay in touch with your parents, whether you are living across the country or just across town. Look at the advantages over old-fashioned letter writing:
- You don't have to waste money on a stamp.
- You don't have to worry about your parents criticizing your poor spelling (so long as you hit the spell check button before you hit the "send" button).
- You don't have to waste tremendous amounts of energy walking all the way out to the mailbox.
- You can write just a line or two (which wouldn't be appropriate in a letter because your dad would complain that you are wasting stamp money).

And E-mail has advantages over speaking with your parents on the phone:

- You won't get stuck with a long-distance phone bill (mostly for calls to home asking for money—how ironic).
- You don't have to hear your dad yell at you because you called collect.
- You can write to your parents at 3 A.M. when you are finished with your homework. (If you were going to call, you'd have to do it before your dad goes to bed at 8:30.)
- They can't shout and yell at you over E-mail. (The worst they can do is write in all capital letters.)

If you don't have a modem on the computer at home, tell your parents it is time for them to move into the 1990s (especially since the rest of society is living in the twenty-first century).

Give Your Parents a Clue

Your parents will want to stay involved in your life, and they'll want to help out and do nice things for you. (Absence makes the heart grow fonder, and all that mush.) But your parents may need a few suggestions of what they can send you. So you don't get stuck with a lot of stuff that you don't want (like socks and vitamins), give them suggestions like:

- *Your hometown newspaper.* Tell your parents that you don't care if the city council approves the zoning for the waste disposal plant, but you *are* interested in articles about your favorite high-school teams and activities.
- *Your magazine subscriptions.* Perhaps your parents won't notice that the postage to send them to you is more than the full cover price of the magazine.
- *Packages filled with goodies.* And here you may wish to specify that your definition of "goodies" includes Oreos and M&Ms but excludes socks and vitamins.

Don't Let This Happen to You

A son who was away at college wrote this cryptic E-mail message to his father in the quest for a little spending money:

"No fun. No mon. Your son."

The father's prompt reply was equally succinct:

"Too bad. So sad. Your dad."

If you are going to ask for money, don't be so crass and blatant about it. At least disguise your request a bit by telling your folks a little about what is happening in your life.

Siblings at Home

As tough as it will be for your parents when you leave home, it could be worse on any younger brothers or sisters that you leave behind. You have been the "big brother" or "big sister" for their entire lives. They have looked up to you (figuratively and literally). Oh, sure, they might have been like little pests for quite a while, but that is only because they were trying to get your attention.

Don't forget to be considerate about the feelings of your younger siblings when you go away to college or move out on your own. They might possibly feel forgotten or unloved. After all, your parents will be making quite a fuss over you. *You* will be getting all of the attention; *you* will be the one who is leaving home on a great adventure; *you* are the one who is taking the extra television set. It's all you, you, you. And what does your kid brother or sister get: nothing but your chores and a set of depressed parents.

With a little planning, you can make the transition a little less painful for your younger siblings. Take the time to:

• Send them e-mails on a regular basis.

- If you're away at college, send them a shirt or cap with the college logo.
- Come home for their birthdays.
- Invite them to spend a day or two living with you.

A little kindness now could reap big dividends in the future. Sixty years from now, you'll be glad that you have younger siblings. Maybe they will come to visit you in the nursing home.

Returning Home

Sooner or later, after you have been away for several months, you will return home for the first time. Maybe it will be over the Thanksgiving holiday. Maybe it will be a Christmas vacation. Whenever that first time arrives, as you walk through the door of your house it will be like stepping into Bizarre-O World.

It won't seem strange at first. There will be the typical greeting rituals. Your mom will kiss you, your dad will hug you, your dog will sniff you, and your little brother will sniff you too. Then you'll throw your trash bag (full of dirty clothes) into the laundry room and move to your room to make a few phone calls to friends you haven't seen.

There! Right at that point, you notice a funny look on your parents' faces. But in ignorant bliss, you make the calls. Another contorted expression appears on their faces when you tell them that you are going out for dinner with friends. Your mother starts whimpering like an injured squirrel. You think to yourself: "Do they *really* think that I am going to spend all of my free time with them?" Well, we are here to tell you: Yes, they do!

Once you realize that you and your parents have opposite expectations, it will be easier for you to negotiate a treaty for peaceful coexistence.

Stepping Back in Time

When you lived at home in the "old days" before you moved away, you were still living under the house rules imposed by your parents on you during high school. One of the reasons you left home may have been to get away from some of those rules. And whether you objected to them or not, you won't be living under anything close to the same rules in a college dorm or in your own apartment.

But your parents still remember those rules, and they still consider them to apply to you when you're back at home (even if the visit is for a few days). And they will just assume that you remember all of the rules, so they won't review them with you ahead of time.

Avoiding Inevitable Conflicts

You will be doing everyone a favor if you go overboard with telling your plans to your parents when you are back at home. Let them know where you are going and who you will be with. Tell them when you plan to be home if you are going out for a night of activities. Let them know if you are planning to eat at home with the family or whether you will be having dinner with someone else. We know this seems a bit extreme, but when you think about it, this is all a matter of courteous communication.

- - - - - - - - - - - - - - - -

There's no place like home.

- - - - - - - - - - - - - - - -

Dorothy Gail, Kansas

Moving On

Moving out on your own is one of the fun aspects about becoming an adult. Another feature of adulthood, less fun at times, is working a job. In the next chapter we'll look at the wonderful world of work that awaits you.

I knew I wanted to serve the Lord and follow His will, but I couldn't decide between majoring in Business or in Religious Studies (to be a youth pastor). Then a friend told me, "We've got a lot of youth pastors, but we could sure use some more Christian businessmen." Then I knew exactly what the Lord wanted me to do.

Jon C., age 24

CHAPTER 10

Jobs and Careers—
So What Are You Going to Do?

Let's play a little *Jeopardy*. Here's the answer:

**It was the best of times,
it was the worst of times.**

Now, what's the question? No, it's not, "What was your last date?" That famous quote is the opening sentence from *A Tale of Two Cities* by Charles Dickens (and you thought you left Dickens behind in high school).

Even though that observation about life was made more than 140 years ago, it easily applies to our world today (hint: good literature is always timeless). At the dawning of the new millennium, you live in a time when it seems things couldn't get any better. Yet some people have decided that current world conditions are on a path to disaster.

If you believe that things in the world are great, then you are an *optimist*. You believe the experts when they tell you the following.

- Prosperity is at an all-time high.
- Poverty is at an all-time low.
- World peace is just around the corner.
- We are protecting the environment better than ever before.
- There is greater opportunity for all.

If you are a *pessimist*, then you believe the experts who make these statements.

- There are more people in poverty than ever before.
- The world is overpopulated and getting worse.
- There is more ethnic cleansing and more wars than ever.
- We have abused the environment to the point that it may not recover.
- Our world is on the verge of economic collapse.

The optimist proclaims that we live in the best of all possible worlds; the pessimist fears this is true.

James Branch Cabell

We're not suggesting that you have to choose one perspective or the other (personally, we prefer an optimistic overview with a healthy dose of pessimism thrown in to make sure we remain compassionate toward others, concerned for the environment, and cautiously optimistic about the future). We just want you to know that you have a choice when it comes to your view of the world. And your view—even though it is only one—really does count.

Your Unique Place in This World

You may be one of six billion people on the planet, but you are significant at a time when your voice can be heard. There may be more people and more problems in the world, but that only means there are more opportunities for you to make a difference.

A hundred years ago you wouldn't have journeyed more than one hundred miles from home in your lifetime, which would have lasted less than fifty years. Today you've probably traveled across the country and maybe overseas, and you plan to live to be a hundred years old (admit it, you want Willard Scott to put you on the Smuckers jar).

Through the camera lens, you've seen people travel to space and plumb the depths of the ocean. You've witnessed the collapse of communism, viewed the wonder of life through a microscope, and studied the vastness of space through a telescope.

The wonders and availability of technology have given you access to sights and information previous generations could only dream about. With the click of a mouse button you can access as much knowledge as you want and virtually go anywhere you desire. And you're just getting started!

What Do You Want to Be When You Grow Up?

If you could take only one thing away from this book, here it is:

Live life on purpose, because there's a purpose for your life.

You're not here by accident. There's a reason for your existence. Your life and what you do really do matter.

You may not always feel like that. Hey, you may not even feel like that now. That's why you just have to believe it's true. But you don't have to take our word for it. Here's what the Creator of the universe, the One who knows you best and loves you most, says:

"For I know the plans I have for you," says the Lord. "They are plans for good and not for disaster, to give you a future and a hope."

JEREMIAH 29:11

Doesn't that give you amazing confidence? Knowing that God has plans for you should empower you as you look to the future and decide what you want to do with your life. You may not be there yet in a literal sense, but you should always be there mentally. Why wait until you graduate from college or get that big break you've been waiting for? *Now* is the time to plan for your future impact.

Living Your Life in Three Tenses

No matter where you are in life, you will always be living your life in three tenses. Here's what we mean:

- You are the product of your *past*, which prepared you for what you are doing now.
- You are experiencing life in the *present* in a very dynamic way as you learn from and interact with others.
- You are hopeful and preparing for the *future*, which includes people you haven't met and experiences you haven't had.

The Antidote to Fear and the Alternative to Pressure

On the one hand, we don't mean to make you nervous about your life right now. We're not saying that you've got to get out there in the real world and make your mark by next week. You're in a period of preparation, and that's going to take a few years.

On the other hand, maybe it's time for you to get out of the nest, which could be home but could just as easily be a comfortable, safe place, like school. Or you could be working in a so-so job you know you don't want to do forever. The fact of the matter is that you're too comfortable and too dependent on others. You might be afraid of what could go wrong if you step out in an attempt to find your place and make your mark in this world.

The Antidote to Fear Is Trust

All of us fear the future to some degree. It's only natural. But you can't let your fear paralyze you. If you want to get things done and find your place, you have to move on. But you're nervous and afraid. What should you do?

The only antidote to fear we have found is *trust*. You have to trust that there will be opportunities for you and your skills. You have to trust other people to respond favorably to your talents and desires. Most of all—since the doors of opportunity sometimes close, and people can and will let you down—you have to trust God.

That's not as difficult as it seems. What you have to do is keep in constant communication by allowing him to talk to you, through his Word, as you talk to him, through prayer (remember the art of spiritual breathing?). You will be amazed how God will guide you to his plans one step at a time.

God's Word is a Lamp, Not a Searchlight

We are so anxious to know everything about our futures, but God knows better. He knows, for example, that if we did know everything, we would either take our eyes off him or run scared. That's why the Bible describes itself as a "lamp" for your feet and a "light" for your path. God will give you just enough illumination for your next step, not the rest of your life.

The Alternative to Pressure Is a Plan

As you step out in faith and find your place in this world, you're going to feel pressure:

- the pressure to find the right job or career
- the pressure to compete once you're in that job or career
- the pressure that you'll make the wrong choice

That's why a plan is so important. If you don't have a plan to get you *somewhere*, you'll end up going *nowhere*. To our way of thinking, the path to your plan involves *work*.

Work Matters

There was a television character on the old "Dobie Gillis Show" by the name of Maynard G. Krebs (played by Bob Denver, who went on to stardom as Gilligan). Maynard was a "beatnik"—forerunner of the hippie, which evolved to the present-day slacker—who went into convulsions every time someone mentioned the word *work*. It was funny (trust us, it was) because Maynard was a funny character who epitomized the idea of getting by with doing as little as possible or nothing at all. As our friend Larry Hopper used to say, "I love work; I could sit and watch it for hours."

Even today, forty years after Maynard, high-school students who are slackers can be funny. But there's nothing even mildly amusing about adult slackers.

Here's the deal. These next few years are going to be the optimum time for you to decide what you want to *do*—which is closely tied to whom you want to *be*. Now, we're not saying that you need to belabor your decision to work part-time at the Gap to pay for books (although your jobs in college can give you a clue to what your long-term aspirations should be). And that's not to say there won't be opportunities for you to change gears later in life—there are forty-year-old housewives who return to school and the work force after spending years at home. But it can get a lot harder, the longer you wait.

If you're heading for college, you have some time. No one is pushing you to chisel out your career path in stone ... yet. On the other hand, if you have opted to skip college and work right out of high school, your situation is a little more delicate. Working full-time pulling down $8.50 an hour is OK— as long as you're living at home or with three roommates. But sometime in the next few years you're going to have to figure out what you want to do for the foreseeable future, if not the rest of your life.

Why Work at All?
OK, we know this isn't the question you're really asking. What you really want to know is, "What's the value of work?" Besides the good things work does for the economy, work is a noble act for human beings. Back when the world was a perfect place, God asked Adam and Eve to "work" in his garden:

> The Lord God placed the man in the Garden of Eden to tend and care for it.
>
> GENESIS 2:15

Even after sin entered the world, work was an important part of the human condition.

> So the Lord God banished Adam and his wife from the Garden of Eden, and he sent Adam out to cultivate the ground from which he had been made.
>
> GENESIS 3:23

Despite what you may think, work wasn't a "curse" then, and it isn't a curse now! Work was a blessing from God to ensure our survival and our well-being. Look at these verses from the Bible about work:

> And may the Lord our God show us his approval and make our efforts successful. Yes, make our efforts successful!
>
> PSALMS 90:17

> Work brings profit, but mere talk leads to poverty!
>
> PROVERBS 14:23

Work hard and cheerfully at whatever you do, as though you were working for the Lord rather than for people.

COLOSSIANS 3:23

And if you need any more convincing that work is important, even God works (although we're not sure if he punches a time clock or not). God created the universe, and when he was done, the Bible says, he "rested from his work" (Gn 2:2).

Ideally, work is a blessing from God for several reasons:

• Work gives you dignity.
• Work creates responsibility.
• Work provides for your family.
• Work gets things done.
• Work honors God.

The Privilege of Work

Notice we said that *ideally* work is a blessing from God. We are very aware that work can discourage and dehumanize people. More than half the world's population lives in poverty, unable to work at a level that gives them dignity, let alone provides for their family. Many lack even the most basic necessities.

If this causes you to stop and think and perhaps even feel a little guilty, that's OK. Later in the chapter we're going to give you some ideas as to how you can do something to help others in need.

For now, let's concentrate on you, because you won't help anyone by sitting around feeling sorry for the world or feeling guilty for living in the most prosperous society on earth. Yes, you are privileged. The very fact that you can read makes you privileged (only 30 percent of the people in the world are literate). The very fact that you have the option to go to college makes you privileged (only 1 percent of people in the world go to college).

Never mind what kind of income you will have in the future. The fact is that you have *opportunity* to work and succeed. That alone makes you privileged. What you need to think about is what you are going to do with what you have. Because you are privileged, are you going to live responsibly before God and the world? Or are you going to squander your talents and resources because your priorities are in the wrong order?

Much is required from those to whom much is given, and much more is required from those to whom much more is given.

LUKE 12:48

Who Do You Want to Become?

You see, from where you are now, ready to begin to prepare for your future career, it's not a question of "What do you want to do?" The question you need to be asking yourself is, "Who do I want to become?"

Write a Personal Mission Statement for Your Life

A lot of career counselors will advise you to prepare a resume. We agree that's important, but we think it's even more vital to write a personal mission statement. We talked about mission statements in Chapter Four, but in case you have forgotten what we said (or had the poor judgment to skip that chapter), here's a quick refresher.

A personal mission statement doesn't have to be complicated—in fact, the simpler and clearer, the better. As an example, here is Stan's personal mission statement, written more than twenty years ago:

"To be an influence to others and glorify God in all I do."

You may want to add a few more details to yours, but don't get too specific. Your mission statement should be a compass, not a road map. You want it to define your purpose for life so you will never forget it.

Yes, you will *do* something. But who you want to become will influence what you will do (or at least it should). Don't get caught in the unfulfilling cycle of pursuing a career or a profession because it offers the most money or the most opportunity for advancement. There's nothing wrong with ambition (in fact, we encourage it), but your ambitions will be more productive and fulfilling if they're plugged into a purpose for your life.

If you base your career ambitions on your purpose for life, you're going to stand out from the crowd. Many people pursue materialism as a motive for working, which is why many people are unhappy in their work.

Our experience is that regardless of the job, career, or profession, the people who are happiest and most fulfilled are those whose work comes out of a sense of who they are and what they want to contribute to the world. Does this mean you need to aspire to be another Mother Teresa, who lived among the poor and the sick in Calcutta? Possibly, but not likely. The more probable scenario for you is that you will end up doing something very ordinary. But it won't be the work that defines you. Rather, you will define your work. And that's what will lift you and your work out of the ordinary to the level of extraordinary.

The Three Bricklayers

Three bricklayers were working side by side on a church construction project. When asked what he was doing, the first bricklayer said, "I'm laying bricks, what does it look like I'm doing?" The second bricklayer said, "I'm laying bricks for this wall, which will be an important part of this building." The third bricklayer replied, "I'm building a cathedral that's going to glorify God."

What Are You Looking For?

Over the next few years, as you find what it is you want to do, you're going to have a choice as to how you look at your work. Are you going to have

- a *job* where you simply earn a paycheck?
- a *career* where you can climb the ladder? or
- a *mission* where you can make a difference in what you do?

The choice is yours. What you have to realize is that God can use you wherever you are, as long as you are available. Like the prophet Isaiah said, "Lord, I'll go! Send me" (Is 6:8).

That doesn't mean that God is going to send you into the deepest, darkest jungles of Brazil ... but it might. It doesn't necessarily mean that you will have to give up your job so you can serve God full-time ... but it might. And it doesn't necessarily mean that you won't have lots of money ... but it might.

Being available to God—whether you are a student, an employee, or an employer—means that you are willing to do whatever it takes and to do whatever he wants. You just need to know that the chances are very good that God will want to use you right where you are to influence the people around you.

Tools to Help You Decide

Nobody—especially God—expects you to walk blindly into a job or career and hope for the best. And nobody—especially us—is telling you that work is so important that it doesn't matter what you do, as long as you're working. Use your head (God gave you a brain so you can think) and your heart. What is it that you really want to do? Who do you really want to become?

But don't just rely on yourself. The bookstores and libraries are full of resources to help you evaluate your skills and match them up with potential jobs and careers. There are some excellent Web sites as well. Here are just a few:

www.careercity.com—This site features job-related information, including resume and interview tips, a searchable jobs data base, and quizzes on various aspects of employment.

www.monster.com—Includes current job listings and a resume posting service, categorized by location and profession.

www.ajob4u.com—Features general information on resume evaluation, career counseling, and job search advice.

Whether you are in school or working for a company, talk to a career counselor who can evaluate your personality and work skills and then match you with an appropriate job or career.

Anyone Can Be a Missionary

Even though God may not call you to be a missionary in the formal sense of leaving home, learning a language, and working with people in foreign countries, it's important that you get involved with missions and ministries.

As every missionary knows, you have to help meet the *physical* needs of people before you can hope to touch their *spiritual* needs. There are four categories of physical needs that people have. Next to each one we have listed a reliable organization that needs your help:

- *Food:* There are many wonderful agencies and organizations that meet this most basic physical need. The world's largest privately funded, faith-based relief and development organization is World Vision (www.worldvision.org).

- *Clothing:* When it comes to providing clothing for people in need, the most visible and reliable organization is the Salvation Army (www.salvationarmyusa.org). It's fine to drop your used clothing at one of their trailers around town, but for a real contribution, volunteer to "ring the bell" for the Salvation Army at Christmas sometime. It will be incredibly interesting and rewarding.

- *Shelter:* One of the most dynamic nonprofit organizations in this country is Habitat for Humanity (www.habit.org), a "nonprofit, ecumenical Christian housing ministry dedicated to eliminating substandard housing and homelessness worldwide." Why does Habitat build homes? "Because of Jesus," says Millard Fuller, the cofounder. "We are putting God's love into action."

- *Work:* There are many ministries that find jobs for persons of disability and for people who have made serious mistakes in their lives and need a second chance. A ministry in our community is Hope Now for Youth (www.hopenow.org). No doubt there is a similar organization in your own city.

You can certainly give money to these kinds of organizations, but an even greater contribution will come when you give your time or the time of the company you will someday work for or own. There is no greater reward than helping and loving others through and with your work.

Vocation Versus Avocation

A *vocation* is a particular job, business, profession, or trade. An *avocation* is something you do besides your job or profession. For most people, their hobby—such as sailing or skiing—is their avocation. Can we issue you a challenge? Don't make your hobby your avocation. Think bigger. Make your avocation something that contributes to the betterment of others. And if you're really clever, you'll work your hobby into your avocation (for example, you could donate your time to teach people with disabilities how to ski).

The Money Factor

Before we discuss money, we want to clarify one thing: money isn't evil. As the Bible says, "the love of money is at the root of all kinds of evil" (1 Tm 6:10), but money isn't evil in itself.

People will do all sorts of nasty things in order to get money. We're guessing that isn't your problem. Like the rest of us, here's where you're vulnerable:

> Those who love money will never have enough. How absurd to think that wealth brings true happiness!
>
> ECCLESIASTES 5:10

It would be good to memorize that verse now. Following the Bible's advice will save you a lot of grief and stress in the future.

While money should not be the number-one factor in your search for a career, it certainly needs to be considered. In fact, at the risk of sounding like we're contradicting ourselves, we advise you to learn as much as you can about money management (start by rereading Chapter Seven in this book). Then, as you search for a career, look for something that can best fulfill your life's purpose while adequately providing for your material needs. If God blesses you with more than you need, invest it wisely in places that pay both spiritual and material dividends.

Work as If God Is Watching (He Is)

Chances are that you have already had at least one job. Before you start your career, you will no doubt have more jobs of varying degrees. And because some—if not all—of these jobs will have nothing to do with your eventual career, you may have a tendency to treat them as mere necessities, not worthy of your absolute best.

As two guys who have worked with and employed plenty of high-school and college-aged people, we can tell you that the person who slacks off in a part-time job at Burger Time is not on the road to a stellar career in aerospace. Conversely, the person who works hard and honestly even in the lowliest job is more likely to succeed in his or her chosen career.

That's because working hard and honorably has nothing to do with the job and everything to do with character. You should want to do your best in all situations, especially if someone is paying you for your work.

Slaves and Masters

The Bible is very specific on this issue of employees and employers (only it refers to them as slaves and masters). Read Ephesians 6:5-9 and you'll discover some principles that will energize you and glorify God, no matter what job you have or whom you employ. *Employees* are to serve their bosses sincerely, work hard, and work with enthusiasm, "as though you were working for the Lord rather than for people" (Eph 6:7). Likewise, *employers* are to treat their employees right, with respect, and fairly—because our ultimate Master treats us all fairly.

It *Is* Who You Know

You've heard the expression, "It's not *what* you know but *who* you know that counts." Don't get carried away, but there is some truth to that statement. Especially when it comes to pleasing your bosses.

Your attitude and willingness to take on new assignments, to go the extra mile, and to take the initiative will get you noticed and promoted. Employers are looking for skilled and knowledgeable workers, but they would much rather have skilled and knowledgeable people who work with industry and integrity.

And if you really buy into the notion that God is watching you as your Ultimate Master, then you just have to trust that he is going to open more doors of opportunity for those who honor God by serving their earthly masters with sincerity, diligence, and enthusiasm.

How to Get a Job and Keep a Job

We mentioned earlier that between us we have hired lots of people. From our perspective, here is some advice on getting and keeping a job.

Getting a Job

A resume is great—and it may get you a job interview—but it's not going to get you a job. The job interview is the key. Here's how you handle it:

1. Be on time.
2. Dress appropriately (better to be too dressed up than too casual).
3. Be enthusiastic and responsive—but don't talk too much.
4. Do a little homework—find out something about the company you want to work for.
5. Ask questions about the company's philosophy or mission statement.
6. Don't bring up money—let them do it.
7. Never talk negatively about your former employers.
8. Thank your interviewer and send a follow-up thank you letter.
9. Follow up by phone within a week if you haven't heard anything.
10. Pray hard.

> ## How to Keep a Job
>
> Getting a job is just one part of the battle. Keeping a job you like is another matter. Here are our tips:
>
> 1. Be on time every day.
> 2. Dress appropriately (better to be too dressed up than too casual).
> 3. Be enthusiastic and responsive.
> 4. Learn all you can about the company and its customers.
> 5. Do your best to fulfill the company's mission statement.
> 6. Don't ask for a raise—let them offer (unless you haven't had a raise in a year or more, in which case it's appropriate to bring it up).
> 7. Never talk negatively about your boss or fellow employees.
> 8. Show appreciation to those you work for and work with and those who work for you.
> 9. Offer to take on extra projects.
> 10. Pray hard.

The Big Switch

Before we move on to a chapter that will dig deeper into this idea of working and living as though God really matters in your life, we want to cover one final point in this chapter on jobs and careers. Here it is.

What if you choose a career, work for a few years, and then decide you want to do something else? What if you end up going to college to become a latex salesman, graduate with your degree in latex salesmanship, and take a job with one of the Big Eight latex companies—only to find out that latex isn't the career for you? What do you do?

While it's not a good idea to jump from job to job (or major to major, for that matter), the worst thing you can do is to continue in a job or a career you know isn't right for you (or worse, isn't honoring to God). This probably won't happen early in your career. More likely, you will feel the urge to switch jobs or careers after you have worked in a particular field for a few years.

On the other hand, the job you started a few years ago—you know, the one you thought was just temporary—may be leading you to bigger and better things. It's not uncommon for a part-time job to lead to a full-time position and eventually a career. That's why you need to treat every job with respect and always do your best. You may end up really liking it, and you want to make sure your boss is impressed with your skills and work ethic.

Whether you switch jobs or keep the one you have, make sure you get plenty of advice and counsel from people who know you and know your career well. That's why it's so important to have at least one mentor who has your best interests in mind.

Most of all, practice the art of spiritual breathing every day. Seek God through his Word and through prayer. Make every effort to please him, and seek his will for your life in all that you do.

Trust in the Lord with all your heart; do not depend on your own under-standing. Seek his will in all you do, and he will direct your paths.

PROVERBS 3:5-6

You Can Always Finish College Later

While we don't suggest that you drop out of school just so you can "pay the bills," we also recognize that there may be circumstances in which you have left school to work, only to find that your job has opened up a whole new world of interest to you. You may even find that you want to go back to school to get your degree in a field that will enhance your new career direction. Many employers will provide the opportunity—sometimes by paying for part of your tuition—for you to complete a college degree. And it doesn't matter how old you are. It's never too late to finish college!

Moving On

Although we hope you have had some fun along the way, we have been talking about some rather serious stuff: your college education, your finances, and your career. But each of these aspects of your life needs to be held in balance, and your balance is maintained only if you have the proper perspective on your life.

In the next chapter we're going to talk about perspective. Specifically, we'll view how you view the world. We'll be asking where you see God in your worldview, and how you see yourself fitting in.

CHAPTER 11

God and Your Worldview—
Can You See Forever?

U ntil now, your life has been a matter of multiple choice. From now on, life will be more like an essay test.

Throughout your life, people have either told you what to do or told you what to think. Don't feel bad. Until now your body and your brain—in that order—have been in development. About all you could handle was multiple choice, whether it was your teachers, your parents, or Gus the policeman giving you advice. Usually the answers were pretty clear so that you could successfully pass the various "tests" in your life and move on to the next level. No one really cared *how* or *why* you knew what you knew (as long as you weren't cheating). They just wanted to know *that* you knew.

Now that you're moving on and possibly moving out, this whole business of *knowing* is going to change. People will still want to know that you know (in other words, you're still going to have multiple-choice tests), but they're really more interested in *how* you know what you know and *why* (that's where the essays come in). In other words, they want to know what you're thinking.

So What Do You Think?

You may be one of the few people your age who really do know what you think and why. This is probably due to a parent or someone very influential in your life who encouraged you to read and explore and ask questions. And when you did ask questions, they took the time to answer. If you don't know what you think and why, it doesn't mean that no one cared about you. They may have tried to tell you stuff, and you just didn't listen. You may be a late bloomer.

Whether you are a thinking person or a late bloomer doesn't really matter. In the next few years you are going to end up in the same spot as everyone else—in front of people who are going to challenge what you believe. These people will be your friends, roommates, fraternity brothers or sorority sisters, professors, employers, and complete strangers. These are the people who will influence you, for better or for worse.

That's why we believe that *now is* the best possible time to figure out *how* you think and *what* you believe.

Your Worldview Is Showing

You and everyone around you have a *worldview.* How do we know that? Well, by most definitions (we like the one given by Dr. Paul Cox), a worldview "gives an overall framework to one's life, thus giving it direction and purpose—whether good or bad." Even the poor slob who says, "Hey, I don't need no stinkin' worldview; I do what I want, when I want it," has a worldview (we don't recommend it, but it's there).

We've written about worldview before in *Bruce & Stan's Guide to God.* We agree with David Noebel, who wrote what we think is the definitive book on worldview, *Understanding the Times.* Noebel writes:

Every individual bases his thoughts, decisions, and actions on a worldview. A person may not be able to identify his worldview, and it may lack consistency, but his most basic assumptions about the origin of life, purpose, and the future guarantee adherence to some system of thought.[1]

This Is Huge

That definition may do nothing more for you than make you yawn, but you need to know that this is HUGE. Your worldview really does matter, and it really does affect the way you think and act.

Look at it this way. You have a limitless number of options available to you each day, and they're all affected by your worldview:

1. Moral decisions

2. Political views

3. Social options

4. Scientific views

5. College selection

6. Career paths

7. Choices of friends

8. Artistic preferences

9. Financial decisions

10. Time management

11. Leisure activities

How do you decide what to do? What is your guiding principle? What is it that's turning your rudder in the right direction and telling your conscience to do the right thing? It's your worldview. That's the thing that's guiding you in your choices, whether you know it or not.

A person's worldview is evident by what one does with his or her life. Life is a sacred trust, and choices must be made in relation to proper purposes, which require a worldview.

Dr. Paul Cox

Door #1 or Door #2

If you're wondering how to come up with a worldview, there are basically two ways to do it. First, you can *inherit* your worldview, which means you believe what your parents believed, which is probably what *their* parents believed. This isn't totally wrong, unless your parents happen to have a faulty worldview (hey, it happens).

The other way to arrive at a worldview is to absorb the ideas and the lifestyles around you, kind of like a sponge absorbs whatever is around it. This method isn't terribly reliable because, like the sponge, you're likely to pick up a lot of unwanted slop.

As we wrote in *Bruce & Stan's Guide to God,* "the best way to develop a worldview is to investigate the options, consider the evidence, and then make an intelligent choice."[2] We're going to reduce your worldview choices to two because, in reality, that's it. Your worldview either includes God or it doesn't. Here are two handy checklists.

A Worldview Without God

- God is not in the picture.
- All things in the world, including humanity, evolved naturally.
- As the highest evolved being, humanity is the measure of all things and the ultimate authority.
- There is no absolute truth; personal choice is what's most important.
- The government is the highest "law," and government can and must decide what's best for people in areas ranging from business to moral behavior.

A Worldview With God

- God is the Creator of and the Supreme Being in the universe.
- God created all things, including humanity.
- Because human beings are created in the image of God, we have dignity and purpose.
- God's revealed absolute truth comes first; we build our personal beliefs and choices around it.
- God has ordained government as a means of keeping order in an imperfect world.

So Many Religions, So Little Time

Sometimes people choose a worldview without thinking about the implications or consequences. If your worldview doesn't include God, it's not enough to say, "I don't believe in God," or even, "I believe in a higher power, but I don't believe the higher power is personally involved in my life or the world." You must also accept the implications and consequences of that worldview.

Although you have the freedom to choose whichever worldview you think is best, we're going to assume for the sake of discussion that you believe in God and that your worldview includes God. So what? What difference does that make in your life? Lots of people believe in God. In fact, there are many different religions that put God at the center of the universe. How do you know which one is true? And in the end, won't all good people go to heaven anyway?

The Big Lie

You're going to hear the "All Dogs Go to Heaven" argument more than you'll hear the argument that God doesn't exist. It's very fashionable in our culture for people to talk about spiritual things. They'll even talk about God, but not the living, personal God who is involved in history and, more specifically, in your life. God is more of a concept or an idea that wouldn't exist unless we invented him. In fact, when you get right down to it, many people believe that we are God and God is us.

This is what we call the "Big Lie," and it's nothing new. Satan used this argument in the Garden when he told Adam and Eve, "You will become just like God, knowing everything, both good and evil" (Gn 3:5).

Adam and Eve bought into the Big Lie, but rather than becoming just like God, they became enemies of God, and so did the rest of the human race, which is why nothing has changed today. Now you'll hear popular "spiritualists" give the same message in books and on talk shows: You are God. What these phonies are saying may be clever and appealing, but it's still the Big Lie.

True Truth

But you know better than that, don't you? You know that in order for something to be true, it must be true for everyone. Truth is not something that's true for you but not for us. The common argument you will hear today is that, even though we have different ideas about truth, it's OK as long as we agree to disagree.

We're not talking about opinions, such as, "I thought the movie was good." That's not truth, because we may not like the movie. Truth goes something like, "If I jump off this ten-story building, I'm going to really hurt myself and probably die." No one can say, "Well, that's your opinion." It's the truth for everyone.

When it comes to God, you must operate in the area of truth, not opinion. Better yet, you need to think about *true* truth, because God is the ultimate source of truth. There will always be other voices—your college professors, the media, your friends, some mystic writer, a guest on Oprah—who will say they have the truth. It will be your job to sort out the voices, which is no easy task. But you must do it, and you must get good at it, for one simple reason: *Your life depends on it!*

Bruce & Stan's Truth Detector

To help you think through this stuff, we want to give you a "truth detector" to help you come to the right conclusion regarding the truth about God. It's not enough to believe there's a God and to say your worldview includes God. Even the demons believe *in* God (see Jas 2:19). You need to make sure you *believe* that God is the ultimate source for truth.

Here are five questions (taken from *Bruce & Stan's Guide to the End of the World*) you should ask about any source of belief before you commit your life to it:[3]

1. *Can I verify the source?* Can I check out the source against other verifiable standards, such as history? Are there people, in both the present and the past, who can testify to its truth?

2. *Can I trust the source?* Is it completely trustworthy in all situations? Has there ever been a time when the source was not true?

3. *Does everyone who goes to the source get the same results?* Is the source objective (which means it's the same for everybody) or subjective (which means it's different for everybody)?

4. *Does the source come with a guarantee?* Is there some way I can know if the source will be true and trustworthy in the future?

5. *Would I stake my life on the source?* Does my belief in the source and its truth lead me to entrust my life to it—both now and forever?

Go ahead. Try asking these questions of any so-called truth sources. You're going to find that nothing and no one stands up to our truth detector ... except for God. He's the only One who gets a perfect score:

1. *God's existence has been verified through the ages.* God is not some passing fad. Millions of people over thousands of years have testified to his existence.

2. *Many people have tried to disprove God's existence, but none has ever succeeded.* In fact, some very committed atheists have been persuaded of God's reality as they tried to disprove his existence.

3. *God does not discriminate.* He never plays favorites (Acts 10:34). God's love extends to all people everywhere (2 Pt 3:9).

4. *The first guarantee God offers is that you will find God if you look for him* (Jer 29:11-13). Believe it. Jesus is God's answer for the sinful condition of the human race (Acts 16:31).

5. *It's up to you to stake your life on the source.* Many people through the ages have chosen death rather than forsake their relationship with God. As far as we are concerned, there's no other source worthy of your life, both now and forever. But that's something you will have to decide for yourself.

Faith Matters

Wouldn't it be great if you could put God under a microscope or view him through a telescope and actually *see* him with your own eyes? Then you could say, "Look, there he is. There's God. Now I believe!"

The truth is, people have seen the *evidence* for God under the microscope and through the telescope. The incredible order and design of our universe—from the tiniest molecule to the most distant stars—point to the existence of a personal, intelligent, loving Designer. The Bible puts it this way:

> From the time the world was created, people have seen the earth and sky and all that God made. They can clearly see his invisible qualities—his eternal power and divine nature. So they have no excuse whatsoever for not knowing God.
>
> ROMANS 1:20

And the very idea that all people everywhere since time began have thought about God (even the atheist thinks about God) indicates that God is there:

> For the truth about God is known to them instinctively. God has put this knowledge in their hearts.
>
> ROMANS 1:19

Still, we've never actually *seen* God, which means that ultimately you have to have *faith* to believe the evidence about God, which comes through nature, through your heart, through the Bible, and ultimately through Jesus Christ.

What is faith? It is the confident assurance that what we hope for is going to happen. It is the evidence of things we cannot yet see.

HEBREWS 11:1

We are made right in God's sight when we trust in Jesus Christ to take away our sins. And we all can be saved in this same way, no matter who we are or what we have done.

ROMANS 3:22

Faith, which is the same as trust, is what ultimately matters. Faith in God through Jesus Christ is what counts. But it isn't a blind faith. It's faith based on evidence.

Be Ready to Give an Answer

As you get out "in the world," whether that's college or a job or just living on your own, you're going to find that your beliefs are going to be challenged by the skepticism and the lifestyles of just about everyone around you. In your classes and in your work you will probably encounter indifference—if not hostility—toward your belief in the one true God (that's why it's so important to surround yourself with Christian friends).

That's OK. Don't be discouraged. God has you there for a reason, and that reason is to represent and glorify him. And don't be offended. The world is hostile to the things of God. The apostle Paul, a brilliant thinker and debater, knew very well how "foolish" the message of the Bible sounds to "those who are on the road to destruction. But we who are being saved recognize this message as the very power of God" (1 Cor 1:18).

You've heard the expression that the best offense is a great defense? When it comes to the things of God, that is true. You don't need to go on the offensive to attack those who don't believe. Simply study the Bible diligently (2 Tm 2:15) and be ready to give an answer if anyone asks you about your faith.

And if you are asked about your Christian hope, always be ready to explain it. But you must do this in a gentle and respectful way. Keep your conscience clear. Then if people speak evil against you, they will be ashamed when they see what a good life you live because you belong to Christ. Remember, it is better to suffer for doing good, if that is what God wants, than to suffer for doing wrong!

1 Peter 3:15-17

"A Ready Defense"

Nobody has spoken personally to more skeptics on college and university campuses than Josh McDowell. As a university student, Josh was skeptical and even hostile toward the claims of Christ. Then a campus group of believers challenged him to investigate the truth. Josh actually was determined to refute the Christian belief system. When he couldn't do it, he ended up becoming a Christian.

Since then Josh McDowell has written several very helpful books about the Bible and its reliability, the historical truth about Jesus and the resurrection, and the uniqueness of the Christian experience. Our favorite book—and we recommend that you buy it—is *A Ready Defense*. You will find it very useful as you get ready to explain your faith.

The Value of Christian Fellowship

It's one thing to study the truth about God on your own and quite another to find other people who are doing the same thing. You need to "fellowship" with (which literally means "to communicate" with) other believers who can encourage you and pray for you (and you for them).

If you are planning to attend a Christian college, it's going to be easy for you to find people who believe the things you believe. If you're going to attend a secular college or university or plan to work on your own, then it's going to take a little effort to find other Christians. Fortunately, there are several outstanding Christian ministries on most college campuses. We recommend the following:

- Campus Crusade for Christ (www.ccci.org)

- InterVarsity Christian Fellowship (www.ivcf.org)

- The Navigators (www.gospelcom.net/navs/collegiate)

- For information on Catholic churches and ministries near you, check out RCNet (www.rc.net).

In addition to the fellowship these campus ministries can provide, it is absolutely essential that you find a local church. Even if you have had a negative experience with church in the past, you need to give church another chance. Realize that the church isn't a building or a program. The church is you and all believers. The Bible says that Christ loved the church and "gave up his life for her" (Eph 5:25).

In his book, *It's Time to Be Bold*, Michael W. Smith gives four excellent bits of advice about the church:

1. "Give the church a chance." Don't let your past negative experiences ruin your chance to worship God and be around other believers.

2. "Find a church that believes the Bible is God's Word." You would think that all churches do this, but it isn't always the case. The easiest way to find out is to sit through some sermons and classes. Like the people of Berea in the Book of Acts, search the Scriptures to see if your church is really teaching the truth.

3. "Meet regularly with a small group of other believers." Even after you begin attending church regularly, find a smaller group within the larger congregation and get to know them. Do a Bible study together and pray with and for each other. Most churches have a network of small groups, so you won't have to look very far.

4. "Don't let anything come between you and your Christian friends." This doesn't mean you isolate yourself from your non-Christian friends. It just means that you find your true friendships among people who think and believe like you do. As the apostle Paul wrote, "Then make me truly happy by agreeing wholeheartedly with each other, loving one another, and working together with one heart and purpose" (Phil 2:2).

Seek This First

Having a worldview with God in it has tremendous implications, not just for your future but for your life right now. You don't just live with that worldview when you go to church or you're around other Christians. It's something that's a part of you every single minute of your life. Sure, you have questions and concerns and worries about what you're going to do both now and in the future. That's normal. But you can't let them dominate your life and hinder your relationship with God. You need to trust that God loves you and cares for you in every detail of your life.

Jesus knew that his disciples had questions and concerns and worries just like you do. That's why he told them:

Why be like the pagans who are so deeply concerned about these things? Your heavenly Father already knows all your needs, and he will give you all you need from day to day if you live for him and make the Kingdom of God your primary concern.

MATTHEW 6:32-33

Having a worldview with God in it means that you live knowing that God is in your world. He's real and active and ready to use you in a powerful way.

Moving On

In this chapter we've asked you to consider what your life would be like without God, and why you're so much better off with God in your worldview and your life. You could say we've given you the *macro* view of God.

In the next chapter—yes, the *last* chapter—we're going to look at the *micro* view of God (no, that doesn't mean God is a tiny speck—that would be you). What we mean by that is we're going to look at what it takes to have a daily, practical, and very real relationship with God. These are the details of your life you can't just push aside. Not if you want your life to be as exciting and effective as it can possibly be.

CHAPTER 12

Those Things You Do—
What God Wants For You

God is a perfect gentleman. He is always available to you, but he won't intrude on you. He waits for you to seek him. That means, of course, that you are going to have to find time for God in the midst of all of your activities. It won't be easy because there will be many things competing for your time: friends, college, job, and, occasionally, sleep.

In the last chapter we talked about how God deserves to have a priority in our lives. In this chapter we'll talk about practical ways that you can make sure that will happen.

Start by Losing Your Parents' Faith

Does the heading to this section shock you? (If you aren't shocked, at least your parents will be.) Let us explain what we mean. For about eighteen years you have been living under your parents' roof and have been abiding (more or less) by their rules. You have adhered to their principles and respected their opinions. Much of what they believe has probably rubbed off on you. You might have even adopted their faith as your own without many questions.

Having your parents' faith may have gotten you through high school, but it won't cut it in the real world after high school. Your beliefs are going to be questioned, challenged, and attacked. If you don't know what you believe and why you believe it, your faith will be crushed.

We aren't saying that you can't have the same faith in God that your parents have. But you need to understand that it has to be *your* faith. Your relationship with God needs to be personal—you and him. You cannot have a relationship with God vicariously (through your parents).

- - - - - - - - - - - - - - - - -
**You won't get to heaven just because
your parents have faith in Jesus.
God doesn't have any grandchildren.**
- - - - - - - - - - - - - - - - -

Staying Connected With God

Suppose that a few years from now you fall in love and become engaged to be married. How would you feel if during the period of your engagement you never received a call or a visit from your future spouse? Oh, there were good intentions to spend time with you, but too many activities got in the way. Well, we all know that your wedding plans would be tossed in the dumpster.

Imagine how God feels when we ignore him. We might have good intentions, but they frequently fizzle out. Do we really expect to wake up at 5 A.M. for a little Bible reading if we were at a party until after midnight? Fortunately, God won't throw us in the dumpster, but we can't expect that our relationship with him will develop if we are continually giving him just the leftovers of our time and energy.

Talking to God

Prayer is nothing more than talking to God. We don't mean that it is an insignificant endeavor. Quite the contrary. Talking one-on-one with the Creator of the universe is a huge deal. But many people get all flustered by it:

- *They think they have to use old-fashioned English phrases.* They throw in a lot of "thee" and "thou" expressions. Basically, they must think that God likes to hear us talk like Shakespeare. Or ...

- *They think they must make their voice sound "spiritual."* All that happens is that they end up sounding like the narrator at the Haunted Mansion in Disneyland. (God isn't scared by it, but we don't think that he wants us to feel obligated to get voice lessons in order to talk to him.) Or ...

- *They think they must engage in some long and protracted soliloquy that reviews the history of mankind and covers all people—living and dead—who have ever populated the globe* (and they must be mentioned by name). If this is your understanding of prayer, then you can only do it if you can spare an entire evening and can talk for several hours without breathing.

Your prayers with God should be like natural conversation: talk to him about what is bugging you; thank him for how he has taken care of you; ask him for guidance in the problem areas of your life.

Just be yourself when you are talking to God, but remember whom you are talking to:

- *Don't treat God like some sort of celestial vending machine* that will drop down from heaven whatever you want.

- *Don't patronize him.* He is not some old, senile, drooling grandfather in the sky. He is not going to fall for your "if I do this for you, then you should do this for me" routine.

- *Be honest with him.* After all, he knows when you are truthful and when you are being hypocritical, so don't try to fake it with him.

The important thing about prayer is that you do it regularly.

Why Do You Need to Say Anything to a Mind Reader?

If God knows everything (and he does), then why should we pray to him if he already knows what we would say? That's a fair question. We think that prayers are for our benefit, not God's. When we pray:

- We remind ourselves that he is in control.

- We acknowledge that he deserves our worship.

- We curb our own pride and independence by submitting our concerns to him.

Listening to God

There are two ways that you listen to God. The first is by being quiet during some of your prayer time. You can't hear God in your thoughts if you are doing all of the talking.

The other way to hear what God says is to read the Bible. After all, those are his words, and they were written for you. We know that Bible reading can seem like a chore at times, but that is usually because people have the wrong attitude about it:

- They think the Bible is an antiquated history book with no relevance for today. Or …

- They think the Bible is full of a bunch of fairy tales and has no relevance for real life. Or …

- They are intimidated by the size of the book—lots of pages, fine print, and no pictures (though sometimes some nifty maps). Or . . .

- They fall asleep while reading it (which usually happens because they are reading at the end of the day when they are in their pajamas and tucked under the covers).

On the other hand, you will find great excitement in the Bible if you consider that it is:

- The "owner's manual" for your life which has been painstakingly written by your manufacturer.
- A true, historical account of intergalactic battles between the forces of good and evil, with *you* as the prize that they are fighting over.
- A success manual for advice and spiritual wisdom in areas of relationships, finance, and employment.
- A guide for the future—your future—that will tell you precisely how your world is going to end and what happens after that.

The important thing about studying the Bible (just like prayer) is that you do it regularly.

How to Get Started

When you begin your new life after high school, you might have great intentions for reading the Bible on a daily basis. If you have never tried this before, then you might want to try a few methods that have proven successful for others.

We suggest you get one of those specialty Bibles that have broken all of the books and verses into 365 daily readings. Each day you have a pre-assigned passage from the Old Testament and from the New Testament. If you miss a day or two, don't give up; just resume with the portion for that particular day. (If you feel compelled to read what you missed, you might quit if you missed too many days in a row.)

Check Out the Body

The New Testament describes the Church as the "body" of Christ. Each follower of Christ is compared to a part in the body of Christ. That analogy tells you two things, but to illustrate them you have to assume that you are the "large intestine" in the body of Christ.

- First, the church won't work properly if you aren't participating. A body needs its large intestine to function properly.

- Second, you won't be spiritually functioning as God designed if you aren't participating in a church. You will be just like a large intestine flopping around all by itself, unconnected to the rest of the body. What a mess.

When you are out on your own, you'll be tempted to skip church from time to time. Don't do it. Get connected with a group of believers so that you are encouraged and held accountable in your spiritual walk.

Which Church Is the Right One?

If you move away from home, you will be faced with the task of finding a church in your new town. There will probably be lots of them to choose from. How do you know which one is right for you? Good question.

Here are a few clues for finding a good church:

- *You might want to start with a church of the same denomination that you attended at home.* Remember that there may be some tough going in your new circumstances, and you may need a place to feel spiritually "at home" even if you are in a new city.
- *Do the church services focus on the Bible?* Does the minister preach from the Bible? Is he interested in the words of God, or is he preaching sermons like "The Importance of a Smile" and "Do Your Part to Prevent Forest Fires"?
- *Is there a family atmosphere in the church?* Are you going to be able to meet and know people at a meaningful level? Your church experience needs to be more than just sitting through a praise chorus concert (although that type of worship is great); you need to be developing deep friendships with other believers.

- *If transportation is a problem, look for a church that has a ministry for college students on your campus.* The chances are good that arrangements for transportation are available. There may be churches that offer Bible studies and other activities on campus.
- *Does the church you are considering offer service opportunities?* As a college student, your life will be lived in a bit of a bubble. In many respects it can be too easy for college students to isolate themselves from the rest of the world. You may be interested in finding a church that gives you opportunities to serve, both at the church and in the community.

An important part about going to church is that you do it regularly. This doesn't win you extra credit with God, but it will help you personally, and your participation will help the other members in your church family.

Finding Christ on Campus

As we discussed in Chapter Two, you will have some interesting challenges if you are attending a secular college or university. If that is the case, then find a Christian group on campus. There are many organizations designed for Christian college students (such as Campus Crusade, Navigators, and InterVarsity, whose Web sites are listed in Chapter Eleven). While these groups don't replace your need to be involved in a church, they are designed to provide you with a Christian support group on campus and in the dorms.

Knowing God's Will

As we spend time talking about issues of the Christian faith with people your age, there is one question that keeps popping up: "How can I know God's will for my life?" That is a great question, and you'd probably like to know the answer to it.

Well, we'd like to give you a definitive answer to it, but we don't have one. The issue of knowing God's will can't be answered simply like a question on "The Hollywood Squares" ("I'll take St. Peter to block"). Between the two of us, we have spent sixty years after high school trying to find God's will. We are convinced that there is no single formula, but we keep learning principles that might be helpful to you in the process of seeking his direction for your life.

Seven Things That Bruce & Stan
Are Learning About God's Will

1. *God isn't trying to play a guessing game with you.* He is not trying to make his will difficult to find. He is anxious for you to know what he desires of you.

2. *Most of the time, there is not one single, overriding plan for your life.* Don't worry that you might guess wrong and get stuck with God's Plan B for your life instead of the better Plan A. Some people fret that if they make one minor misjudgment of God's will, then they will be off track for the rest of their lives. (Example: "Oh, what if I should have taken the World Civ course instead of Psychology? What if the person God wanted me to marry was in the World Civ class? Now I will never meet that person, and I'll get stuck marrying somebody else.") Think about it. Before the world was created, God knew what choices you would make. He is not going to be surprised by what you choose, and he can work the circumstances around your choices.

3. *There are a lot of areas where God's will doesn't matter.* For example, we don't think he particularly cares what breakfast cereal you choose or which parking space you select.

4. *God's will has momentum.* It seems that he moves us along in the direction that we are supposed to be going. Drastic changes at the spur of the moment are possible in God's will, but it seems he usually goes with a more methodical approach. (Example: Before he calls you to be a missionary in China, he might have you working in a cross-cultural ministry in your hometown.)

5. *God equips you for doing his will.* He has given you a specific personality and spiritual gifts. He has given you certain aptitudes, talents, and skills. Don't you think it is likely that his will for your life is going to involve your unique characteristics?

6. *Prayer plays a big part in knowing God's will.* Remember that prayer involves *listening* to God as much as it does *talking* to him. Don't expect to hear a James Earl Jones–type voice booming down from heaven. Instead, allow God to direct your thoughts in the quietness of your prayer time with him.

7. *God's will isn't so much a time or a place or a person.* It is primarily a condition of your heart. God wants you to be willing to serve and follow him. He wants you to be moldable and moveable. You should spend your time working on your relationship with God, and let him be responsible for arranging the circumstances of your life to guide you where he wants you to be.

Here's an amazing thought: Everything you need to know about God's will is in the Bible. Now, don't panic. It is not revealed in some secret, obscure verse in Habakkuk that you have never read (although there are probably quite a few verses in Habakkuk that you might have never read). Nope. It is right there in plain view in the New Testament:

> Jesus replied, "'You must love the Lord your God with all your heart, all your soul, and all your mind.' This is the first and greatest commandment. A second is equally important: 'Love your neighbor as yourself.'"
>
> MATTHEW 22:37-39

There it is! That's God will for you—that you love him and that you show love to those around you.

We can almost hear you thinking, "It can't be as simple as that!" But it is. If you are actively involved in knowing and loving God, and if you are obeying him, then you are doing his will for your life.

A Final Word (Actually, Quite a Few of Them)
About Keeping Christ Preeminent in Your Life

We think it is very appropriate that the *last* section of this book is a discussion about putting Christ *first*. (After all, Christ said, "The last shall be first." But we realize he wasn't talking about this book.) But it is not just our opinion that Christ should have first place in your life. The Bible says so.

> Christ ... is first in everything.
>
> COLOSSIANS 1:18

As we have described throughout this book, your life after high school is going to be hectic. Your schedule is likely to be over-committed with many things. You'll be busy will college, friends, jobs, and activities. These will all be *good* things, things that have merit and are worthwhile. That is exactly why you will have difficulty learning how to keep your life in balance. Sometimes you'll have to make a choice between several things, all of which are good.

In setting the priorities of your life, remember that God deserves first place. Your life will be out of sync if you relegate him to any other position.

How Does "Keeping Christ Preeminent" Work on a Practical Level?
This is the million-dollar question. Earlier in this chapter we reviewed some of the specific things you can do: prayer, Bible study, and worship with other believers. Now, as we conclude this book, we want to give you a few guidelines that may help you to conceptualize the whole process of keeping Christ in first place in your life.

First, let's mention a few misconceptions about faith:

- *"Keeping Christ preeminent" is not the isolation of your faith from life.* Too many people treat their faith as if it is in a box. They bring out the box on Sundays and religious holidays. The rest of the time, it sits on the shelf and has absolutely no relationship to their everyday life. For them, their faith is totally isolated from real life. It is only a meaningless ritual. But God did not intend for our faith to be merely decoration or an ornament that we look at but don't touch. He wants our faith to influence and energize our lives. Jesus said,

> "My purpose is to give life in all its fullness."
>
> JOHN 10:10

- *"Keeping Christ preeminent" is not the indoctrination of faith for life.* Some people mistakenly believe that their faith cannot withstand critical analysis by the secular world. Their faith is precious to them, so they don't want to expose its weakness to attack. They approach faith as if it is something to be memorized but not analyzed. They know what they believe but not why they believe. They have a "bomb shelter" mentality about their faith: they'll stay indoctrinated in their belief, but they will avoid any dialogue with skeptics because they can't imagine that any logical, rationally thinking person would really believe this stuff. These poor people are missing out on the assurance and confidence that comes from *knowing,* without any doubt, that Christ is the truth.

> Jesus told him, "I am the way, the truth, and the life."
>
> JOHN 14:6

They are held captive by their fear that their faith cannot survive critical thinking. But the faith is shallow because it has only been memorized. It is in their heads only, not their hearts. They could be truly free if they really knew and understood the truth:

> Jesus said to the people who believed in him, "You are truly my disciples if you keep obeying my teachings. And you will know the truth, and the truth will set you free."
>
> JOHN 8:31-32

- *"Keeping Christ preeminent" is not the intersection of faith with life.* Don't mislead yourself by thinking that Christ has first place in your life just because you occasionally bring him into some of the events of your life (like praying before you take a college test or before your performance review at work). And don't think you are giving him the highest priority just because you don't swear, drink, or do other "bad" things. (There are a lot of atheists who don't swear and drink.) God should be much more involved in your life than just making a few "guest appearances" in some of your activities. We make the mistake of reserving him for the really tough times, for the emergencies, or as a matter of last resort. We often fail to consider him as being relevant to all aspects of our lives. But that is a huge mistake on our part. God is totally relevant, always available, and wholly capable for each and every circumstance of our lives.

> As we know Jesus better, his divine power gives us everything we need for living a godly life.
>
> 2 PETER 1:3

You cannot live your life to its fullest if you only give Christ limited access to it.

"Keeping Christ Preeminent" Is the Integration of Faith and Life

We've been looking at those circumstances when Christ is not in first place. Now let's see what a life is like when he is given top priority.

We give Christ first place when we give him access and control of all areas of our lives. We just don't treat him as a religious lucky charm that we keep for decorative more than functional purposes. Our faith in him should affect *what* we do and the *way* we do it.

We believe life only makes sense from his perspective. Because he is the truth, life without God doesn't make sense. Regardless of the skeptics, Christ reigning preeminent in our lives gives us total assurance. We can have faith in our faith.

We allow the Holy Spirit to influence our total beings. We become different—as college students, as employees, and as friends—when all areas of our lives are permeated with him. The apostle Paul said it very succinctly:

> Whatever you do or say, let it be as a representative of the Lord Jesus.
>
> COLOSSIANS 3:17

That one verse sums it up very nicely. Christ is preeminent in your life only when he is glorified by everything you say and do.

Moving On

Up until this page, we sent you to the next chapter whenever you came to this "Moving On" section. Now it really is time for you to move on ... past the back cover of this book and into real life.

We are sincerely excited about what lies ahead for you in your life after high school. Yes, there will be a mix of thrills and tragedies, but we are confident that you are going to find adventure in all of the experiences that are part of your new responsibilities and freedom.

We like the way Peter ended his first epistle to the Christians in Asia Minor:

My purpose in writing is to encourage you and assure you that the grace of God is with you no matter what happens.

1 PETER 5:12

That is how we feel about this book and you. We hope you have been encouraged to step boldly into life after high school with the realization that God wants to lead you in that journey.

NOTES

Chapter 2
College—Growing Smarter by Degrees

1. Robert C. Kallgren and Bryan E. Beyer, "Bible Breath: Too Much?" from *Today's Guide to Christian Colleges* (Barrington, Ill.: Real Media Group, 1999), 15.

Chapter 5
Friends—Choose or Lose

1. Alan Loy McGinnis, *The Friendship Factor* (Minneapolis, Minn.: Augsburg, 1979), 22.
2. James R. Gimbel, ed., *The Campus Connection* (St. Louis, Mo.: Concordia, 1998), 18.

Chapter 6
More Than Friends—Dating and Beyond

1. Neil Clark Warren, *Finding the Love of Your Life* (Wheaton, Ill.: Tyndale, 1992), 53.
2. James Dobson, *Life on the Edge* (Nashville, Tenn.: Word, 1995), 102.

Chapter 8
Healthy Choices—Preparing Your Body to Last a Lifetime

1. Christopher D. Hudson, ed., *College Clues for the Clueless* (Uhrichsville, Ohio: Promise, 1999), 198.
2. Cheryl Townsley, *Food Smart* (New York: Jeremy P. Tarcher/Putnam, 1997), 92.
3. Stormie Omartian, *Greater Health God's Way* (Eugene, Ore.: Harvest House, 1996), 138.

Chapter 11
God and Your Worldview—Can You See Forever?

1. David Noebel, *Understanding the Times* (Eugene, Ore: Harvest House, 1991), 1.
2. Bruce Bickel and Stan Jantz, *Bruce & Stan's Guide to God* (Eugene, Ore.: Harvest House, 1997), 107.
3. Bruce Bickel and Stan Jantz, *Bruce & Stan's Guide to the End of the World* (Eugene, Ore.: Harvest House, 1999), 58.

BIBLIOGRAPHY

Bickel, Bruce and Jantz, Stan. *Bruce & Stan's Guide to God*. Eugene, OR: Harvest House Publishers, 1997.

Bickel, Bruce and Jantz, Stan. *Bruce & Stan's Guide to the End of the World*. Eugene, OR: Harvest House Publishers, 1999.

Biehl, Bobb. *Mentoring: Confidence in Finding a Mentor and Becoming One*. Nashville, TN: Broadman & Holman, 1997.

Covey, Stephen R. *The Seven Habits of Highly Effective People*. New York, NY: Simon & Schuster, 1989.

Dobson, James. *Life on the Edge*. Nashville, TN: Word Publishing, 1995.

Harris, Joshua. *I Kissed Dating Goodbye*. Sisters, OR: Multnomah Books, 1997.

Hudsen, Christopher D., ed. *College Clues for the Clueless*. Uhrichsville, OH: Promise Press, 1999.

Gimbel, James R., ed. *The Campus Connection*. St. Louis, MO: Concordia Publishing House, 1998.

Kallgren, Robert C. and Beyer Byran E. "Bible Breath: Too Much?" from *Today's Guide to Christian Colleges*. Barrington, IL: Real Media Group, 1999.

McDowell, Josh and Wilson, Bill. *A Ready Defense*. Nashville, TN: Thomas Nelson Publishers, 1993.

McGinnis, Alan Loy. *The Friendship Factor*. Minneapolis, MN: Augsburg Publishing House, 1979.

Noebel, David. *Understanding the Times*. Eugene, OR: Harvest House Publishers, 1991.

Omartian, Stormie. *Greater Health God's Way*. Eugene, OR: Harvest House Publishers, 1996.

Smith, Michael W. *It's Time to Be Bold*. Nashville, TN: Word Publishers, 1997.

Townsley, Cheryl. *Food Smart*. New York: Jeremy P. Tarcher/Putnam, 1997.

Warren, Neil Clark. *Finding the Love of Your Life*. Wheaton, IL: Tyndale House Publishers, 1992.

Worthington, Janet Farrar and Farrar, Ronald. *The Ultimate College Survival Guide*. Princeton, NJ: Peterson's, 1998.